"Lorraine Varela is a gifted w
the Face of ISIS is a challenge to ......ned,
to pray fervently for our brothers and sisters abroad and to
practice Christlike grace and truth—even when confronting
the darkest of foes."

Lela Gilbert, author and journalist, Jerusalem, Israel

"*Love in the Face of ISIS* is an inspiring read, a reminder that
the perfect love of God casts out all fear. This book encourages
readers to pray strategically for ISIS and the persecuted
Church in the Middle East—obeying our Lord Jesus Christ's
words to love our enemies and to pray for those who persecute us. Already the Lord has been hearing and answering
our prayers. We have multiple testimonies of Muslims encountering a Man in white in their dreams, of Saul-to-Paul
encounters, of Muslims becoming followers of Christ who,
because they have been forgiven much, love much—even unto
death! It is an exciting time of revival, with a harvest of souls
by the power of the Holy Spirit, with love bringing them
from a kingdom of darkness into the Kingdom of Light so
that Jesus' name is above all names. This is a must-read! You
will be encouraged to join the army of radical lovers and
intercessors by joining with the great Intercessor!"

Samaa Habib, author, *Face to Face with Jesus*

"Not only does this book give an accurate historical and
political account of the crisis in Iraq. But it is a book about
the profound love of G-d, which can and will change everything. The love of G-d brings light into absolute darkness.
It changes and transforms individual lives. This is a book
that can change your life."

The Reverend Canon Dr. Andrew P. B. White, president,
Foundation for Relief and Reconciliation
in the Middle East (FRRME)

"*Love in the Face of ISIS* is a call to the war room of prayer. Jesus and His disciples constantly call us not to fear, but to walk confidently forward in faith. When disaster strikes, we are not called to gather food and guns and head for the bunker; we are to go into the storms to rescue those who are lost. . . . If you are grieving over the victims of ISIS, read Lorraine's book. If you are challenged by Jesus' admonition to pray for your enemies, read Lorraine's book. If you would like to send financial support to those suffering from the Middle East crisis, listen to Lorraine. She's been there and knows some of the people. If you feel that your prayers need jump-starting to the next level, or if you want to have some model prayers that can be lifted to the heavens in Jesus' name, read and respond to Lorraine's call to action."

from the foreword by Don Finto, founder
and director emeritus, Caleb Company;
author, *Your People Shall Be My People*

Love in the face of ISIS

Seven Prayer Strategies for
the Crisis in the Middle East

LORRAINE MARIE VARELA

Chosen
a division of Baker Publishing Group
Minneapolis, Minnesota

© 2016 by Lorraine Marie Varela

Published by Chosen Books
11400 Hampshire Avenue South
Bloomington, Minnesota 55438
www.chosenbooks.com

Chosen Books is a division of
Baker Publishing Group, Grand Rapids, Michigan

Printed in the United States of America

Library of Congress Control Number: 2016930595

ISBN 978-0-8007-9800-0

Cover design by Gearbox/Dan Pitts

16 17 18 19 20 21 22   7 6 5 4 3 2 1

This book is dedicated to the memory of
all the courageous men, women and children
of the Middle East
who loved the Lord
and followed Jesus, even unto death—
and for their families who remain,
who love them still

Who shall separate us from the love of Christ?
Shall tribulation, or distress, or persecution, or famine,
or nakedness, or peril, or sword?

As it is written:

"For Your sake we are killed all day long;
We are accounted as sheep for the slaughter."

Yet in all these things
we are more than conquerors
through Him who loved us.

For I am persuaded that
neither death nor life,
nor angels nor principalities nor powers,
nor things present nor things to come,
nor height nor depth,
nor any other created thing,
shall be able to separate us
from the love of God
which is in Christ Jesus our Lord.

ROMANS 8:35–39

Contents

Foreword

I am honored to write a foreword for Lorraine Varela's *Love in the Face of ISIS*. One of the top reasons I am honored is that Lorraine's pastoral leader, whom I trust, was the first person to call my attention to this book. Lorraine is respected in her community of believers. That commands my respect. Another reason is Lorraine's grasp of the subject. She has visited with some of those most affected in this evil war zone and is showing us the Jesus way to respond.

From the time I picked up Lorraine's book and began to read, I was captivated by her insights into the challenges faced by those in the wake of ISIS, but I was also encouraged by her loyalty to the Word of God and the Spirit of Jesus.

Jesus told us to love our enemies and to bless those who persecute us. These are not just nice words for church liturgy. Jesus is calling us to a lifestyle, a lifestyle that many of our brothers and sisters being tortured and often killed for their faith are demonstrating, and the only lifestyle that will conquer evil and call millions into the Kingdom.

Love in the Face of ISIS is a call to the war room of prayer. Jesus and His disciples constantly call us not to fear, but to walk confidently forward in faith. When disaster strikes, we are not called to gather food and guns and head for the bunker; we are to go into the storms to rescue those who are lost.

"Do not be anxious about anything," Paul wrote from a Roman jail, "but in every situation, by prayer and petition, with thanksgiving, present your requests to God" (Philippians 4:6 NIV). Only then does God's peace prevail.

Not only is ISIS displaying the grossest evil on the world stage, but it is also televising some of today's strongest saints. The Lord wants all of us to learn the lesson: Even in the midst of persecution and martyrdom, His way works! Love conquers! The apparent winner is not always the real winner. Those who have died often produce a harvest of souls. The Gospel of Jesus is more powerful than the strongest enemy. Many young Muslims are turning away from Islam and to Jesus because of the atrocities being paraded. They are turning from a god of hatred and destruction to a God of love and acceptance. Lorraine understands this and is calling the Church to move against the tide of fear and hate into the battle with love and prayer. Remember the promises! Pray for His presence—in the lives of both the killer and the killed. Pray for an increase of dreams and visions through which multiple thousands are turning to Jesus.

In Jesus' parable of the wheat and the weeds, He told His friends that both righteousness and wickedness would ripen side by side as we move toward the final great harvest at the end of this age. Our propensity is to focus only on the rise of wickedness. Lorraine reminds us that as the bad news, the darkness, deepens, the light will grow stronger.

We Bible readers often quote the words of Revelation 12:11, that we overcome the enemy "by the blood of the Lamb and by the word of [our] testimony," but we may not always include the last phrase, "They did not love their lives so much as to shrink from death" (NIV).

If you are grieving over the victims of ISIS, read Lorraine's book. If you are challenged by Jesus' admonition to pray for your enemies, read Lorraine's book. If you would like to send financial support to those suffering from the Middle East crisis, listen to Lorraine. She's been there and knows some of the people. If you feel that your prayers need jump-starting to the next level, or if you want to have some model prayers that can be lifted to the heavens in Jesus' name, read and respond to Lorraine's call to action.

Don Finto, founder and director emeritus, Caleb Company;
author, *Your People Shall Be My People*

Acknowledgments

This book was a miracle in the making from start to finish. I am delighted to give credit where credit is due! And so, with heartfelt appreciation, I say "Thank you" to:

My husband, Gabriel, who has supported me through every step of this process, from the beginning of this assignment to our unforgettable journey through Jordan—you caught the vision and made it your own. This book is the fruit of your efforts as well.

My parents, Glenn and Tamara Unfreid, who taught by example how to pray without ceasing, covering me daily in prayer.

My faith-filled partners at Chosen Books, who saw value in these words and opened the doors, bringing *Love in the Face of ISIS* to life: Dwight Baker, Kim Bangs, Jane Campbell, Carra Carr, Erin Hollister, Steve Oates, Jim Parrish, Dan Pitts, Natasha Sperling and Shaun Tabatt.

My friends on the frontlines who bring hope to the hurting, who shared their stories with me: Andrew White, Connie Wilson, Sarah Ahmed, Hanna Ishaq, Richard and Christy Sherrod, Joel and Heather Quinones from FRRME; Jeremy Courtney, Cody Fisher and Matt Willingham from PLC; Jonathan and Ann Webb from ICF.

My prayer team, family, Pastors Hylan and Rita Slobodkin and Beit Tikvah community, who constantly encouraged me through prayers and words of life. I cherished every word.

My beloved Jesus, for depositing Your book into my spirit and making my heart like Yours.

Introduction

Why Love?

Love in the face of ISIS.

This phrase seemed to come out of nowhere as it connected deeply with my spirit. A moment earlier I had been focused on worship, surrounded by my congregation as we sang to the Lord. I knew immediately it was a word from God—and I knew it was to be His title for this book.

It was a hard word to receive. The very premise assaulted my emotions with the conflict it presented and the answer it implied. I began to pray and ask the Lord why He chose these words for the title.

Instead He asked me, "What is love? *Who* is love?"

It was then I realized the significance of these words.

God, who is not only the source of love but who *is* love, inserted Himself into this conflict by directing my attention back to Him. As I substituted His character attribute of love with His name, the title read *God in the face of ISIS.*

That is powerful!

Setting Your Eyes on Jesus

As you begin to take up this assignment to pray over the crisis in the Middle East, it is crucial that you keep your eyes focused on the One who is Love, and not let your heart become weighed down by the horrific forces of evil. Through prayer, you are able to assume an offensive position to defeat the enemy as you come into agreement with the purposes of God—the God of love, of mercy and of justice.

God reveals Himself through His various names and titles throughout Scripture to direct your attention to His character. Each name and title complements the others to give deeper insight as you discover the nature of the One you serve. Here are a few of the ways He makes Himself known through His name:

The Lord Is There (see Ezekiel 48:35)

The Lord of Hosts (see Isaiah 47:4)

The Lord Is My Shepherd (see Psalm 23:1)

The Lord Is My Banner (see Exodus 17:15)

The Lord Will Provide (see Genesis 22:14)

The Lord Who Heals (see Exodus 15:26)

The Lord Is Peace (see Judges 6:24)

Each one of these attributes is meaningful and necessary as you use your authority as a believer to pray over the situation in the Middle East. In chapters 3 through 9, you will find strategic guidelines on how to pray through these seven names of God and release His purposes to meet the needs of those who have been—and those who are—persecuted for the sake of the cross.

God also manifests Himself through His Son, Jesus, who is God incarnate, God in the flesh. Each name and title of

God was fulfilled in the life of Jesus when He came to earth. Scripture reveals Jesus as:

God with Us (see Isaiah 7:14)
The Power of God (see 1 Corinthians 1:24)
The Good Shepherd (see John 10:11)
The Deliverer (see Romans 11:26)
The Bread of Life (see John 6:35)
The Resurrection and the Life (see John 11:25)
The Prince of Peace (see Isaiah 9:6)

It is through the name of Jesus that God comes to bring life to all who will call upon Him. His name brings light to darkness, setting captives free. His name is majestic in all the earth, and His name is Lord of all.

The name of Jesus is the name above every other name—*far* above the name of ISIS.

Who Is ISIS?

On June 10, 2014, ISIS—the Islamic State of Iraq and Syria—stormed onto the world stage through its hostile takeover of Mosul, Iraq, a city of more than one and a half million people. As jihadists, with their black flags, advanced on the city, the Iraqi army turned and fled for its life, leaving behind an arsenal of weaponry and military machinery as spoils for the militants as well as a city wide open for a brutal attack. By the end of the day, the borders of Mosul were flooded with 150,000 people attempting desperately to leave the city and find safety[1]—numbers that would grow rapidly, as more than 600,000 people took flight.[2]

This was just the beginning of the torment and chaos. Within the month, the Islamic extremists targeted the Christian population of Mosul, demanding that believers convert to Islam and pay a religious tax (called *jizya*) for alleged protection to stay, or else leave the city and thereby forfeit everything they owned. Christians who refused these options "will have nothing left but the sword," read the ISIS statement, a threat made by letter that was also broadcast via loudspeakers from mosques for the people to hear.[3]

To mark Christian-held property, an Arabic letter that stands for the word Nazarene (*Nasrani* is a pejorative term in Arabic for *Christian*) was spray-painted onto the homes and businesses of those known to believe in Jesus.[4] With the deadline for the ultimatum fast approaching, most Christians who had initially remained in Mosul now chose to flee. Some fled on foot to the nearest town of Qaraqosh eighteen miles away, many with just the clothes on their backs.[5]

It was not always this way.

Christianity thrived in Iraq for two thousand years, ever since the apostle Thomas arrived to bring the good news of the Gospel to the people of this historic, biblical region. Iraq—home of the ancient civilization of Mesopotamia and later the Assyrian and Babylonian kingdoms—was the birthplace of Abraham, the land of exile for Ezekiel and Daniel, and the mission field of Jonah the prophet who brought God's message of repentance to Nineveh, now known as the city of Mosul.

It is in Iraq that the Tigris and Euphrates rivers flow with life, and it is there that one day a highway will be built for the Egyptians and Assyrians to worship the Lord, joining with Israel to be a blessing in the earth (see Isaiah

19:23–25). Israel is the only nation that has more biblical history and prophecy recorded in Scripture than the nation of Iraq.[6]

But within this land of future peace and unity, recent decades have witnessed unimagined violence. The Islamic State of Iraq and Syria has not concealed its desire to rid the Middle East of Christians and the influence of Christianity. By doing so it is following in the footsteps of successful campaigns, including pogroms, that have purged many Middle Eastern nations of their Jewish populations. In 1948 Iraq had a vibrant Jewish population numbering 150,000. By 2013 fewer than a dozen aging Iraqi Jews remained. Most traces of Jewish people living in Iraq have all but disappeared.[7]

In the same way, in 1947 Iraq had a thriving population of some 4.7 million Christians. At the start of the Iraq war in 2003, the Christian population was estimated at 1.5 million people. By 2013 that number had dwindled to 300,000. Since ISIS swarmed in to establish its self-proclaimed caliphate in June 2014, a record 125,000 Christians fled within the first twelve months, leaving only an estimated 175,000 Christians. And their numbers continue to decrease.

It is not just Christians who are targeted, however. Within the borders of Iraq and Syria, ISIS continues to persecute, torture and kill those of any faith that do not adhere to its extreme ideology—including other Sunni and Shi'a Muslims.

In August 2014 more than 35,000 Yazidi people—a religious minority group that blends elements of Christianity, Islam and the ancient Persian faith of Zoroastrianism—were forced to flee to Mount Sinjar or face slaughter by ISIS troops.[8] ISIS massacred more than two thousand men through horrific deaths on the mountain, while many of the women and girls were forcibly taken as wives and slaves. It was a humanitarian crisis that drew the world's shocked attention to ISIS once again.

The swift mobilization of ISIS has given a clue to its deeper roots. This new enemy has been revealed as the resurgence of an old adversary: al Qaeda. That earlier terrorist regime, led by Osama bin Laden, struck fear in the hearts of Americans with the attacks of September 11, 2001, killing nearly three thousand people and catapulting America into a decade-long war on terror.

ISIS has, in fact, changed the face of terrorism. Determined to establish an Islamic caliphate—territory dominated by the spiritual head of Islam and Muhammad's successor—ISIS has utilized highly visible acts of barbaric violence, doubling as a recruitment tactic to attract a flood of new jihadists, many from foreign countries.[9] Through its brazen declaration on June 29, 2014—"The Caliphate is established!"—ISIS accomplished what other radical Islamic factions had only dreamed to do, thereby demanding the allegiance of Muslims worldwide.[10]

ISIS, the richest terrorist organization in history,[11] promotes its own brand of utopian society through media-savvy propaganda, keeping its goal firmly in sight: to cleanse the world of all who disagree with its ideology.

Love Overcomes Evil

Twenty-one Egyptian Coptic Christians were marched to their deaths in February 2015. Hooded ISIS captors cloaked in black led the Christian men dressed in orange jumpsuits, hands bound behind their backs, along the sandy beach at the ocean's edge. Their gruesome executions were captured on a video that carried these words: "A Message in Blood to the Nation of the Cross." The kingdom of darkness was sending a challenge to the Kingdom of light. And as with the kingdom conflict culminating two thousand years ago in Calvary's cross, darkness thought that it had won.

The ISIS message was strong in images and in words—a message rooted in deception, justifying the beheadings of Christians who "have been carrying the cross delusion for a long time, filled with spite against Islam and Muslims."[12] If these captors had known the One who is Love, they would have recognized that to their last breaths these people of the cross lived out a very different message—a message Jesus taught them: to love your enemies, bless those who curse you, do good to those who hate you and pray for those who spitefully use and persecute you. A message that love is stronger than hate, that good overcomes evil.

Darkness did not win. It was at the cross that Jesus disarmed principalities and powers, making a public spectacle of them (see Colossians 2:15). Love triumphed over death. Love triumphs still. Jesus said, "These things I have spoken to you, that in Me you may have peace. In the world you will have tribulation; but be of good cheer, I have overcome the world" (John 16:33).

What is love? Love is giving. Love is serving. Love is sharing with those in need. Love is carrying someone else's burden as you lift that one up in prayer. Jesus said, "Greater love has no one than this, than to lay down one's life for his friends" (John 15:13). Love is an active, tangible demonstration of God's heart on display.

As love comes to stand in the face of ISIS, you can partner with the purposes of God. Love your brothers and sisters as

Your First Line of Defense

They came first for the parents, with a terrifying demand.

"Either you say the words and convert to Islam, or we will kill all your children."

Forcing their way into the home of a Christian family living in Iraq, ISIS militants stood ready to act on their threats.

It was more than the father could bear. In desperation, he said the words the militants wanted to hear . . . and the lives of his children were spared.

Consumed with anguish, the father wondered if Jesus would love him still.

They came back for the children. But this time, the brutality became more unspeakable.

Turning to the children, the threat was repeated.

"Say the words that you will follow Muhammad," the ISIS terrorists demanded.

The children refused.

They loved Jesus. They had always loved and followed Him. They knew His love and presence.

"Say the words!"

Once again the children said no. Their love for Jesus never wavered.

They loved Jesus to the end.

Overcoming Helplessness

Testimonies that arise from the crisis facing those living in the Middle East are too horrific in scope to comprehend fully. Men in orange jumpsuits awaiting execution, women and girls forced into sexual slavery, children beheaded for their faith—you grieve over the pain, the injustice, the terror and the torment inflicted on these innocent men, women and children.

As the stories unfold and the atrocities worsen, your inability to intervene could lead to frustration and eventual feelings of helplessness. *But are you helpless?*

Not according to the Word of God! Consider these promises:

> The effective, fervent prayer of a righteous man avails much.
>
> James 5:16

> For whatever is born of God overcomes the world. And this is the victory that has overcome the world—our faith.
>
> 1 John 5:4

> "For the eyes of the LORD are on the righteous, and His ears are open to their prayers."
>
> 1 Peter 3:12

Let us hold fast the confession of our hope without wavering, for He who promised is faithful.

Hebrews 10:23

But know that the LORD has set apart for Himself him who is godly; the LORD will hear when I call to Him.

Psalm 4:3

"It shall come to pass that before they call, I will answer; and while they are still speaking, I will hear."

Isaiah 65:24

Let us therefore come boldly to the throne of grace, that we may obtain mercy and find grace to help in time of need.

Hebrews 4:16

For all the promises of God in Him are Yes, and in Him Amen, to the glory of God through us.

2 Corinthians 1:20

Thank God that prayer is not your last resort when all else fails—it is to be your first line of defense in times of trouble.

Fixing Your Eyes on the Promises of God

Surrendering to the influence of your emotions over the truth of God's Word is a dangerous practice. In doing so you play into the schemes of the enemy, who attempts continually to divert your attention away from the promises of God and the power that is released when you agree with Him in prayer.

It is ingrained into human nature to trust what your eyes can see. You rely on your natural senses to give information from which you make logical conclusions. But faith does not originate with what you can see in the natural realm.

When God steps in and gives you a directive with a promise, He invites you to place your faith in a higher realm than the one you inhabit—a realm where His power and authority reign. He invites you to place your trust in Him.

This is where faith is born.

Joshua and Caleb were two young men who understood this Kingdom principle. Born into slavery in Egypt, they were led out of slavery with the children of Israel during the miraculous exodus by the hand of God.

For more than one year, the children of Israel witnessed signs, miracles and wonders that proved God's power and His love for them.

When they needed direction, the Lord led them with a pillar of cloud by day and a pillar of fire by night. When their enemies surrounded them, God made a way of escape as He parted the Red Sea, leading them on dry ground to safety. When they were hungry, God sent bread from heaven to feed them.

Now Joshua and Caleb, along with ten others, were given the directive to spy out the land of Canaan, which God had promised to give to the people of Israel.

For forty days, the twelve men spied out the land of promise. They saw with their eyes that the land was exceedingly good. They also saw that the people of the land were strong and their cities well fortified.

When they returned to give their report, ten of the men had their eyes fixed on the impossible situation that loomed in front of them. But Joshua and Caleb had their eyes fixed on the Lord:

> "The land we passed through to spy out is an exceedingly good land. If the LORD delights in us, then He will bring us into this

land and give it to us, 'a land which flows with milk and honey.' Only do not rebel against the LORD, nor fear the people of the land, for they are our bread; their protection has departed from them, and the LORD is with us. Do not fear them."

Numbers 14:7–9

Sadly, the people agreed with the majority position and turned their hearts away from the promise of God.

The spies who brought back the evil report about the land died by plague, and the children of Israel wandered for forty years until the generation that had been freed from slavery died in the wilderness. Only Joshua and Caleb entered into the Promised Land with the generation that followed (see Numbers 14:20–38).

God was looking for those whose hearts were in alignment with His.

He is still looking for hearts like these—people of faith who have the confident expectation that He is faithful to His word and He will act, even if it cannot be confirmed by what they see or feel.

Reconnecting with the Heart of God

So where is the disconnect? If you have faith in God above your own natural circumstances, and you believe in the promises He has made to you, then why do your prayers sometimes *feel* ineffective and powerless?

You need to begin by understanding what prayer *is* and what prayer *is not*.

- Prayer is the noblest form of speech; it is not meaningless words spoken through repetition or ritual.

- Prayer is a life-giving form of communing with the living God; it is not a one-way monologue.
- Prayer is mindful acknowledgment of God, which engages both soul and spirit; it is not thoughtless habit performed out of duty or obligation.
- Prayer is our agreement with the plans and purposes of God; it is not a demand to have our own way.

When you pray, you unite your heart with God's heart. Releasing the concerns of your heart, you place them into His capable hands. While you wait for the release of His answer to be fulfilled, you rest securely in Him.

Rest—the place of victory and peace.

In rest, the enemy cannot touch you because you are surrounded by God's presence. Rest is not passive! When you rest in God, there is ongoing strengthening and renewal as His life flows to you. Rest is a tool that builds you up with courage and strength.

Out of this place of rest, your faith is renewed to believe in His promises, His purposes and His timing for the release of directives and answers from heaven.

Engaging in Prayer through Worship

Worship is the foundation for your time in prayer. It is the greatest gift you can give to the Lord, for how can you commune with God and not engage your heart in worship?

Worship sets the Lord first, above everything else. Worship requires your time and attention. Worship engages your affection. Worship demands the intentional surrender of your desires in exchange for His.

Consider this simple method as you come to the Lord in prayer:

P: Posture yourself for worship

R: Remove all distractions

A: Adore the Lord

Y: Yield to His desires

When I use the word *posture* above, I am referring to the position of your heart. It is an attitude of undivided focus that brings you into agreement with the Lord and the desires of *His* heart. This focus releases awe in your inner man. Within this place of reverence and wonder, His wisdom will flow to you and fill you with all you need. "Oh come, let us worship and bow down; let us kneel before the LORD our Maker. For He is our God, and we are the people of His pasture, and the sheep of His hand" (Psalm 95:6–7).

The Tools of the Trade

A young woman hobbled down the jetway, her legs unsteady as she prepared to board our plane for her very first flight. Once seated, she could not stop the violent tremors that shook her body.

In my job as a flight attendant, I had worked with many types of people, but I had never seen anyone so consumed by fear.

Noticing her discomfort—in fact, she began crying out to deplane—our crew asked a sympathetic pilot who was traveling as a passenger to sit in the seat next to her and help calm her nerves. With each sound and movement of the plane, the pilot explained the mechanics of flight and began to dispel her fear with information. His technique worked.

Anxiety produces the fruit of doubt—doubt that challenges the truth of God's Word; doubt that influences your decisions; doubt that works in opposition to faith. It is no wonder that Scripture says to be anxious for nothing!

> Be anxious for nothing, but in everything by prayer and supplication, with thanksgiving, let your requests be made known to God; and the peace of God, which surpasses all understanding, will guard your hearts and minds through Christ Jesus.
>
> Philippians 4:6–7

The apostle Paul gives us the tools to overcome anxiety in this order—prayer, supplication and thanksgiving. Prayer opens the door to commune with God. Supplication releases your humble request, allowing an opportunity for you to share the concerns of your heart, listening for the comfort of His response. This interchange creates a well of thanksgiving to overflow in your spirit. It is God's will that you give thanks. Your spirit is built up as you come into agreement with the Spirit of God. Thanksgiving is a powerful tool.

Thanksgiving is also a powerful weapon that helps to defeat the purposes of the enemy.

In 2 Chronicles 20, we read that multiple armies came to do battle with Jehoshaphat, the king of Judah. Jehoshaphat's response was to seek the Lord. Jehoshaphat bowed himself down in worship, and all of the people followed his example.

When the armies went out to battle, Jehoshaphat appointed people to sing praises to the Lord. These singers went in front of the army to prepare the way, saying: "Give thanks to the LORD, for His steadfast love endures forever" (2 Chronicles 20:21 ESV).

This probably was not the frontline of defense Israel's enemies were expecting to see. As soon as God's people began to worship, the Lord set an ambush against their enemies. Their adversaries were routed, and Judah was left to collect the spoils.

When you enter into battle in prayer over the Middle East, remember your weapons of thanksgiving and praise. Your eyes will be taken off the temporal circumstances that surround and threaten to overwhelm you, and your vision will be placed in the heavenly realm, where His dominion and rule triumph over every purpose of the enemy.

Persistence Pays Off

And. How often this word is overlooked—a little word that can hold so much importance. "And he told them a parable to the effect that they ought always to pray and not lose heart" (Luke 18:1 ESV). This word *and* signals that the parable Jesus is about to tell is connected to the teaching He has just given to His disciples about the Kingdom of God.

The Jewish religious leaders began by asking Jesus when the Kingdom of God would come. They did not understand that Jesus had already brought His Kingdom into their midst, as their eyes could not see this Kingdom reality that faced them. Every time Jesus healed the sick, cast out demons and performed miracles and signs before their eyes, the Kingdom of God had come to them. Turning to His disciples, Jesus provided them with deeper understanding of His Kingdom— a description of the unmistakable signs of His return when His Kingdom would be fully established (see Luke 17:20–37).

It is following this dialogue that Jesus told the parable of the persistent widow to teach His disciples another Kingdom principle—one that would have profound implications in the final days leading up to His return:

> He said, "In a certain city there was a judge who neither feared God nor respected man. And there was a widow in that city who kept coming to him and saying, 'Give me justice against my adversary.' For a while he refused, but afterward he said to himself, 'Though I neither fear God nor respect man, yet because this widow keeps bothering me, I will give her justice, so that she will not beat me down by her continual coming.'"
>
> Luke 18:2–5 ESV

A widow was one of the most vulnerable people in society.[1] She had a valid case before the judge—he just did not want to be bothered with her situation. She went to him again and again to protect and defend her, so that justice would be executed on her behalf.

Beginning in the first verse, this passage uses three descriptive words to illustrate the nature of persistence in prayer and its eventual result. First, Jesus used the word *ought* to emphasize the need to pray. This Greek word *dei*[2] is not a suggestion. It combines the necessity of prayer with the duty to pray.

How often are you to pray? Always! *Always?* Jesus recognized that this command for continuous prayer can be an overwhelming thought in opposition to human nature. The phrase *lose heart* is translated from the Greek word *ekkakeo* which means "to faint, to be utterly spiritless, to be wearied out or exhausted." Prayer should not have this emotional or physical effect!

Whenever God gives you a command to obey or an instruction to follow, He provides you with the resources you need to see it through: "May he equip you with all you need for doing his will. May he produce in you, through the power of Jesus Christ, every good thing that is pleasing to him" (Hebrews 13:21 NLT).

So pray always! Keep your heart and mind open and alert to what the Lord is doing. Stay sensitive throughout your day to the leading and inner promptings of the Holy Spirit. Keep a ready yes in your heart that responds positively when God requires your time to be spent in His presence. Let your agreements be in keeping with the revealed will of God and Word of God. *Always.*

When the widow persisted, her demands for justice were eventually granted. Why? The unrighteous judge did not want her actions to beat him down. The word used in the text here is *hypopiazo*, which means "to beat black and blue, like a boxer that buffets his body, to wear one out." There was physical discomfort associated with her unrelenting insistence for a righteous ruling.

Jesus uses the example of an unrighteous judge's actions to demonstrate *how much better* the heavenly Father is as the righteous God. "Will not God give justice to his elect, who cry to him day and night? Will he delay long over them? I tell you, he will give justice to them speedily" (Luke 18:7–8 ESV). He tells us here that God is not reluctant to respond to the prayers of His people. That is great news! Persistence in prayer is not an attempt to change God's mind about something He is unwilling to do, but rather a partnering together in agreement with His will to see His purposes released on the earth.

Why then is there a need to persist in prayer if God is already willing? Is not God powerful to act whenever and however He wants? Yes! Of course! Scripture says, however, that "we do not wrestle against flesh and blood, but against principalities, against powers, against the rulers of the darkness of this age, against spiritual hosts of wickedness in the heavenly places" (Ephesians 6:12). Spiritual opposition from the enemy fights against the purposes of God as they are released on the earth.

For three weeks Daniel was in mourning over a prophetic word that had been revealed to him; he "set [his] heart to understand" (Daniel 10:12) and humbled himself in prayer and fasting. From the moment his prayers were spoken, God released the answer—but the answer did not arrive immediately on earth. For 21 days, the messenger of God who was sent to give Daniel revelation was held back by "the prince of the kingdom of Persia," a spiritual ruler of darkness (Daniel 10:13). As Daniel persisted in prayer, the angel Michael was released to help in the spiritual battle until breakthrough happened—and this impressive messenger with a "face like the appearance of lightning, his eyes like flaming torches" came to Daniel with the word of the Lord (Daniel 10:6 ESV). Daniel's persistent prayers joined together with the will of God to release victory over the enemy.

These are the days leading up to Jesus' return, when His Kingdom will be fully established. Each day that passes brings Him one day closer! And in these days, God has not forgotten His people and their cries for help from the adversary of their souls. As ISIS continues to expand its evil practices throughout the Middle East, join your voice with those of your brothers and sisters to cry out to God for His justice to be released. This is an act of obedience that releases faith and is pleasing to Him (see Hebrews 11:6). Jesus concludes His teaching on the Kingdom of God by saying it is so: "And will not God give justice to his elect, who cry to him day and night? Will he delay long over them? I tell you, he will give justice to them speedily. *Nevertheless, when the Son of Man comes, will he find faith on earth?*" (Luke 18:7–8 ESV, emphasis added).

Developing the Heart of an Intercessor

In a world far away from the Middle East, I was raised in a household of faith. As a child I often spent my evenings with my family as we read the Bible aloud, followed by long times of prayer on our knees. Everyone was expected to participate. I learned to take prayer seriously, even if I did not enjoy the exercise or fully appreciate its importance.

One night our family devotions followed the lighthearted reading of the children's classic "Little Red Riding Hood." Unable to distinguish reality from fiction, I was consumed with worry over the thought of this little girl walking into danger, oblivious to the threat of "the big bad wolf" waiting at her grandmother's house.

I identified with her predicament. Our family was enjoying a weekend retreat in the mountains of California, staying the night at my grandmother's cabin in the woods. *This could happen to me!*

I knew that prayer held the answer to my fear.

As our family knelt in front of my grandmother's couch, soon my turn came to pray. With heartfelt sincerity, I began to ask Jesus to protect Little Red Riding Hood from the big bad wolf. The giggles and laughter that flooded the room alerted me to the fact that my prayer was amiss, and my mother gently explained why.

Though my prayers were misguided, in that moment the heart of an intercessor was ignited—a heart that began with the identification of another person's need.

As you turn your heart to pray and intercede for our brothers and sisters in the Middle East, it is easy to allow the enormity of their suffering to turn you away from identifying with their pain. Their reality is not your own, so how could you even begin to empathize with their sorrow? Is it not enough that you are committed to praying for them?

In Romans 12:15 we are reminded to "Rejoice with those who rejoice, and weep with those who weep." Though you may be separated by physical distance, you can allow yourself to weep as the Holy Spirit invites you to share in their burdens.

These are not tears of pity or a forced emotional response. That would be counterproductive as the focus then becomes centered on you.

Rather these tears are given by the Holy Spirit as you join in the intercession He is making on your behalf: "Likewise the Spirit also helps in our weaknesses. For we do not know what we should pray as we ought, but the Spirit Himself makes intercession for us with groanings which cannot be uttered" (Romans 8:26).

Do not be afraid of your emotional response when tears do come. The intensity of emotion might take you by surprise if you have never experienced this type of intercessory prayer. These tears are a gift to help you in your intercession before the Lord.

Through these tears, you will feel a piece of His heart in a way words could never describe. You might need to find a private location where you are free to cry and weep. Remember, though, that these tears are not born out of defeat but victory.

Jesus also offered up prayers and supplications with "vehement cries and tears to Him who was able to save Him from death" (Hebrews 5:7). He who knew the end from the beginning was one with the Father before time began. His cries ensured the victory that was won on the cross, as He became "the author of eternal salvation to all who obey Him" (Hebrews 5:9).

Finding Hope

Without a doubt, the thought of praying for the crisis in the Middle East can be daunting. It takes only a cursory glance at the evening news to be reminded of this fact.

That is why you can be thankful that "with God nothing will be impossible" (Luke 1:37). He loves to meet you in your impossible situations and demonstrate His loving power!

Simon Peter was a fisherman who faced an impossible situation (see Luke 5:1–11). He had been out fishing in his boat all night, doing all the right things—fishing in the right places, at the right time, with the right equipment, just as he had done many times before—but he came up empty-handed, not a single fish for all his efforts.

Tired and frustrated, Peter was on the shore taking care of his nets when a Man got into his boat nearby.

The Man said to Peter, "Let Me use your boat."

The Man was Jesus.

Jesus had been speaking to a crowd of people that had gathered around Him near the shore to hear His words of life. Jesus got into Peter's boat and asked him to "put out a little from shore." Peter did as Jesus asked. Then Jesus sat down and taught the people while in the boat.

When Jesus finished His teaching, He turned his attention to Peter and told him, "Now row out to deep water to cast your nets, and you will have a great catch."

The impossible situation now faced Peter once again. He knew from his experience there were no fish to be caught.

It should have been Peter who first thought up these oft-quoted words: "The definition of insanity is doing the same thing over and over and expecting different results."

Surely to go back to the same place with the same method meant another failure just waiting to happen. *But this time, Jesus was in his boat.* And because of his faith in the word Jesus gave him, Peter came into agreement with this plan and did as Jesus suggested.

The impossible became possible.

The fishing nets teemed with a catch so great that the nets began to break, and Peter's boat began to sink.

Awestruck by the miracle he had witnessed, Peter pulled his boat to shore, left everything behind and followed Jesus.

As you begin to pray and intercede for all those who are being persecuted for their faith in the Middle East, you can look at this impossible situation and take hope. Jesus is in your boat.

Sitting across from you, He steadies His gaze and locks His eyes onto yours. He does not come to remind you of your past failures but to give you hope for your future successes—if you will trust Him and put your faith in His promises.

As you face this impossible situation in prayer, Jesus will show you what to do. He will release the strategies He has prepared to bring the victory. Only believe.

Releasing the Authority and Power of Heaven

What does it mean to release the authority and power of heaven? Does God need your prayers, or does He act as He pleases? Does evil have free rein to exert influence over people, or can your intercession affect its impact on the hearts of others? And if prayers spoken in agreement with God really can make a difference, what is your responsibility in prayer to influence the outcome of affairs on the earth?

The answers to these questions are revealed as you understand the authority a believer is given through prayer, the responsibility a believer holds in prayer and the power that is released when a believer's prayers are in alignment with the will of God.

The Believer's Authority in Prayer

In the beginning . . . man had it so good. The world was created by the Word of God (see John 1:1–5). A beautiful Garden was given as God's provision to man: a sanctuary, a place to experience life with his Creator, a place where all his needs were met. This perfect place was destroyed by an imperfect choice, when man allowed the temptation of his heart to overrule the direct command of God.

God gave dominion—meaning *supreme authority*—to Adam, the first man, to rule over all the earth (see Genesis 1:26). There was just one condition. One! Within the Garden, Adam and his wife, Eve, could eat from any tree except the Tree of the Knowledge of Good and Evil. If they ate from this tree, they would "surely die" (Genesis 2:17).

The serpent came to introduce doubt, which directly opposed the command of God: *"Did God actually say . . . ?"* (Genesis 3:1 esv). The entertainment of that one thought led to an agreement with the idea—and agreement with the idea became an action that defied God's instruction. With just one impulsive and reckless decision, man gave away his supreme authority over the earth to the serpent.

Thousands of years later, the serpent resurfaced as the devil in the wilderness to flaunt the authority he had won in the Garden, tempting Jesus with the premature release of His rightful inheritance—for Jesus had the promise of God that was written in the Psalms: "The Lord has said to Me, 'You are My Son, today I have begotten You. Ask of Me, and I will give You the nations for Your inheritance, and the ends of the earth for Your possession'" (Psalm 2:7–8).

Knowing this promise, the devil showed Jesus "all the kingdoms of the world in a moment of time. And the devil said to Him, 'All this authority I will give You, and their glory; *for this has been delivered to me*, and I give it to whomever I wish. Therefore, if You will worship before me, all will be Yours'" (Luke 4:5–7, emphasis added).

It was not an empty promise. Jesus knew the devil had this authority in his grasp. Instead Jesus submitted to His Father's will, demonstrating the correct response when faced with temptation: He allowed the command of God to overrule the temptation of His heart.

Jesus answered, "Get behind Me, Satan! For it is written, 'You shall worship the LORD your God, and Him only you shall serve'" (Luke 4:8).

Agreement with God is so important! Jesus demonstrated the correct response to the devil's temptation in the wilderness: agreement with the Word of God. Authority that had been lost by man in the Garden would be restored to Jesus after He went to the cross.

Satan has not lost his power . . . *yet*. Power is the ability to control or influence. The battle that exists between God and Satan is not a power struggle. Each has power.

This is a battle for authority, for it is authority with power that Satan craves. Authority directs the use of power. Power is under subjection to authority. A soldier might have an arsenal of weapons at his disposal, but if he does not have the authority to use them in a given situation, his power is rendered ineffective.

Satan is still trying to steal back authority he lost on earth. He does this through agreements people make with him. Whenever a person comes into agreement with Satan's thoughts over God's directives, authority shifts hands—just as it did in the Garden of Eden. When Satan has authority combined with power, he is able to keep people enslaved in bondage and evil is unleashed.

Scripture teaches that the authority of Jesus is carried in the power of His name (see John 14:13). When a person turns to Jesus and believes on His name, that person is saved—and the release of Jesus' authority defeats the power of the enemy over his or her life.

> And Jesus came and spoke to them, saying, "All authority has been given to Me in heaven and on earth. Go therefore and make disciples of all the nations, baptizing them in the name of the Father and of the Son and of the Holy Spirit, teaching them to observe all things that I have commanded you; and lo, I am with you always, even to the end of the age."
>
> Matthew 28:18–20

As a believer in Jesus, you carry His name and you carry His life (see Romans 8:10–11). You are His ambassador, His representative in this world. He has given you His authority and the power of the Holy Spirit to do His works, bringing His Kingdom to earth as it is in heaven (see Luke 9:1–2). These are His works: to destroy the works of the devil (see 1 John 3:8).

When you release the authority of Jesus into a situation by your agreement with His Word in declaration and in prayer, you engage in doing His works as well. It is crucial that you know who you are and the authority you carry to release His works effectively in the earth!

The Believer's Responsibility in Prayer

One day when Jesus had finished praying, His disciples came to Him with a simple request: "Lord, teach us to pray" (Luke 11:1).

The first thing to notice in this passage is that Jesus was someone who prayed (see Luke 5:16). He cultivated a lifestyle of continuous prayer (see John 11:41–42). It would be pointless for Jesus to teach His disciples to pray if prayer were just an exercise in futility. Jesus not only modeled a life of prayer but also placed the responsibility to pray on those who followed Him.

Jesus responded to His disciples, "When you pray, say: Our Father in heaven, hallowed be Your name. Your kingdom come, Your will be done on earth as it is in heaven" (Luke 11:2).

This prayer is an active declaration of your agreement with the purposes of God—an agreement that releases God's will on earth as it is in heaven. If God is going to act with or without your prayers, then this declaration is useless. In his book *Intercessory Prayer* (Regal, 1996), Dutch Sheets teaches that it is obedience to God that brings a response from Him and faith in His Word that releases the power of heaven.

Prayer is a believer's responsibility . . . it is also a privilege and a joy.

The book of Esther chronicles the story of a young Jewish woman living in exile in a foreign land who was given the opportunity and responsibility to save her people from annihilation. With her name changed and her identity hidden, Esther gained favor with the king and was elevated to a position of royalty by becoming his wife. When a plot was uncovered to destroy all the Jewish people in the land, Esther was positioned perfectly to intervene.

Esther had a choice. She could break the law and approach the king without having been summoned—an action punishable by death—or she could turn away and say nothing. It was the advice of her cousin Mordecai that persuaded Esther to take action:

"Do not think in your heart that you will escape in the king's palace any more than all the other Jews. For if you remain completely silent at this time, relief and deliverance will arise for the Jews from another place, but you and your father's house will perish. Yet who knows whether you have come to the kingdom for such a time as this?"

Esther 4:13–14

In the same way, all believers today have the opportunity and the responsibility to come before the King and cover their brothers and sisters in prayer, especially those who are facing persecution, imprisonment and death. Here are some important reminders on the believer's responsibility to pray:

Now I beg you, brethren, through the Lord Jesus Christ, and through the love of the Spirit, that you strive together with me in prayers to God for me, that I may be delivered from those in Judea who do not believe.

Romans 15:30–31

And take the helmet of salvation, and the sword of the Spirit, which is the word of God; praying always with all prayer and supplication in the Spirit, being watchful to this end with all perseverance and supplication for all the saints.

Ephesians 6:17–18

For I know that this will turn out for my deliverance through your prayer and the supply of the Spirit of Jesus Christ.

Philippians 1:19

Remember the prisoners as if chained with them—those who are mistreated—since you yourselves are in the body also.

Hebrews 13:3

Finally, brethren, pray for us, that the word of the Lord may run swiftly and be glorified, just as it is with you, and that we may be delivered from unreasonable and wicked men; for not all have faith.

2 Thessalonians 3:1–2

In prayer you are able to "bear one another's burdens, and so fulfill the law of Christ" (Galatians 6:2). The word used here for "bear" is *bastazo*, which means "to take up in order to carry or bear, to put upon one's self (something) to be carried; to sustain, uphold, support." You do not merely come alongside your brothers and sisters who have burdens; rather, you lift the burdens off their shoulders and place them onto your own, as you sustain and support them in a time of need. What a beautiful description!

When you bear another's burdens, you provide strength and comfort to the one who is weak. It is an obligation for those who are strong to "bear with the failings of the weak, and not to please ourselves" (Romans 15:1 ESV).

Jesus said, "Come to Me, all you who labor and are heavy laden, and I will give you rest" (Matthew 11:28). You co-labor with Jesus when you bear the burdens of your brothers and sisters, because we are one Body in Christ and individually members of one another (see Romans 12:5). Jesus said that we would not only do His works but also do greater works when we ask in His name (see John 14:12–14).

Even Jesus received help to carry His own burden as He was led away to be crucified. "Now as they came out, they found a man of Cyrene, Simon by name. Him they compelled to bear His cross" (Matthew 27:32). The cross was lifted up and placed onto Simon's shoulders as he followed behind Jesus to the place of crucifixion, so that he might sustain and support the One who would die in his place. This was a prophetic act that pointed to the words Jesus had spoken in Luke 9:23–24: "If anyone desires to come after Me, let him deny himself, and take up his cross daily, and follow Me. For whoever desires to save his life will lose it, but whoever loses his life for My sake will save it."

Simon had to be compelled to carry the burden of Christ. Will the same be said about you?

The Believer's Power in Prayer

British Prime Minister Winston Churchill descended fifty feet belowground to the bombproof Operations Room, headquarters of the British Royal Air Force (R.A.F.) No. 11 Fighter Group in command of 25 aircraft squadrons. The date was September 15, 1940.

World War II was well underway. Germany had already conquered Norway, Holland, Belgium and France. For more than two months, the *Luftwaffe*, the German air force, had waged an air campaign against the R.A.F. over the skies of Great Britain.

As Churchill later recounted in his book *Their Finest Hour* (Rosetta, 1949), the weather on that Sunday seemed "suitable to the enemy," so he went to the command post in anticipation of what might lie ahead. On their descent to the two-story Operations Room below, the air marshal in command of the forces told the prime minister, "I don't know whether anything will happen today. At present all is quiet." Within fifteen minutes, German planes were detected on the move. A chain of events that culminated in a decisive victory for the Allies had begun.

Churchill watched as the light bulbs on an enormous blackboard showing R.A.F. squadron availability began to glow. Below him, he saw the large-scale map table surrounded by military personnel feverishly moving disks about to indicate the position of enemy fighters and the movement of Britain's own squadrons to meet them in the air. Soon the lighted blackboard indicated that the majority of R.A.F. squadrons were engaged in a fierce battle.

Until this point Churchill had watched in silence. Now he spoke. "What other reserves have we?"

"There are none," replied the air marshal.

Churchill looked grave. As he later said, "The odds were great; our margins small; the stakes infinite."

Within five minutes, most of the R.A.F. squadrons in the air were forced to land in order to refuel. On the ground and unprotected, the pilots and flight crews had little defense against the enemy, whose assault was certain.

Miraculously, at this moment when the R.A.F. was at its weakest, the German pilots turned from the scene of the battle and retreated. No new attacks surfaced, and within another ten minutes all action had ceased. By the end of October, the Battle of Britain had been won.

The battle was not won by military strength alone, nor was it a matter of fate that turned the tide. Divine intervention was at work, as many believers were praying throughout the battle. In Wales at this time, God raised up a group of intercessors led by a man named Rees Howells who prayed in faith daily that God would turn an impossible situation into victory. Their approach in this military crisis more than seventy years ago is pertinent for us as we watch and pray about the crisis in the Middle East today.

"Nothing was left to chance or a shot-in-the-dark type of praying," explains Norman Grubb in his book *Rees Howells Intercessor* (CLC, 1952):

Everything was examined in God's presence and motives were sifted until the Holy Spirit could show His servant intelligently that there was an undeniable claim for prayer to be answered. Then faith would stand to the claim and lay hold of the victory; and there would be no rest until he had God's own assurance that faith had prevailed and victory was certain. It was not just praying and then *hoping* for an answer.

Look at some of the timeless insights Rees Howells offered:

"Must we have fear because others have fear?"

"We need a real foundation for our faith."

"Can we trust Him for the impossible?"

"The important thing is to find out where God is in this."

"If God is going to deliver from this hell, there will have to be some power released."

"This peace the Savior gives is not an artificial one. It is so deep that even the devil can't disturb it."

"You can't hear things in the Spirit while you have any turmoil or fear in you."

"You can't take fear into the presence of God."

"How could we get victory for the world unless we had first believed it for ourselves?"

Rees Howells and the intercessors who joined him knew they were at war in the physical realm, but they also recognized that their supreme conflict was rooted in the spiritual realm: "For we do not wrestle against flesh and blood, but against principalities, against powers, against the rulers of the darkness of this age, against spiritual hosts of wickedness in the heavenly places" (Ephesians 6:12). The Greek word for *wrestle* occurs just this once in Scripture, and it means "a contest between two in which each endeavors to throw the other, and which is decided when the victor is able to hold his opponent down with his hand upon his neck." This supreme conflict ends when "He has put all enemies under His feet" (1 Corinthians 15:25).

Howells and his intercessors did not trust in what their eyes could see but in the truth of what their hearts had known—the promise of the exceeding greatness of God's power to those who believe:

> That you may know what is the hope of His calling, what are the riches of the glory of His inheritance in the saints, and what is the *exceeding greatness of His power toward us who believe*, according to the working of His mighty power which He worked in Christ when He raised Him from the dead and seated Him at His right hand in the heavenly places, far above all principality and power and might and dominion, and every name that is named, not only in this age but also in that which is to come.
>
> Ephesians 1:18–21, emphasis added

Satan falls like lightning when believers go out in the power of Jesus' name to defeat the works of darkness (see Luke 10:17–18). As Dutch Sheets explains in *Intercessory Prayer*, the devil has already been defeated at the cross; you "re-present" the victory of the cross when you release His mighty power through your agreement with His Word in prayer.

Ananias was a disciple that the Lord used to demonstrate this powerful principle. In a vision, the Lord spoke to Ananias and commanded him to go to a man called Saul of Tarsus. Ananias was to place his hands on Saul, that he might receive his sight (see Acts 9:1–19).

Saul easily fits the profile of a jihadist today—only instead of participating in a holy war to defend Islam, Saul was zealous for his faith in the God of Abraham, Isaac and Jacob. Having consented to the death of Stephen by stoning, "Saul was ravaging the church, and entering house after house, he dragged off men and women and committed them to prison" (Acts 8:3 ESV).

While Saul was breathing threats and murder against believers, the Lord encountered him with His mercy. On his way to Damascus to take more prisoners, Saul was overcome by a light from heaven shining around him, and Jesus spoke audibly to him in the presence of those who accompanied him. Blinded by the light, Saul was led on into the city where he stayed for three days in this condition, neither eating nor drinking. During this time, the Lord gave Saul a vision in which he saw a man named Ananias come to him and restore his eyesight.

This was not an easy assignment for Ananias to accept. He had heard many reports about the harm Saul had done in Jerusalem and knew that Saul had come to Damascus with authority from the chief priests to arrest believers there as well.

The Lord had a different plan for Saul, and Ananias was a vital part of it. Ananias needed a supernatural infilling of God's love in order to love his enemy and release God's healing to Saul, a demonstration of love in action.

In obedience to the command of God and in agreement with His word, Ananias found Saul and called him brother.

He explained that Jesus had sent him so that Saul could see again and be filled with the Holy Spirit.

Ananias—whose name means "the Lord's gracious gift"—placed his hands on Saul as he "re-presented" the victory of Jesus that was won at the cross, releasing His mighty power through agreement with His word that was received in prayer. Saul received his sight immediately.

As a believer in Jesus, you have received the same power of the Holy Spirit (see Acts 1:8). It is your responsibility to release His power through prayer on a consistent basis (see Ephesians 6:18), not only during times when you feel like it or when it is convenient. Prayer is an intentional, purposeful act. Your agreements with God are powerful!

The Highest Name

For centuries God allowed His people to live in a country far away from His land of promise. Egypt, initially a refuge from famine, became the hostile land of their captivity. Generations lived and died in bondage to slavery.

In Moses, God raised up a deliverer to lead the children of Israel out of captivity and into freedom. When Pharaoh refused to let the Israelites go, God confronted the authority and power of the Egyptian gods through devastating plagues. Each plague represented a deity that the Egyptians worshiped. After many of the plagues, Pharaoh relented and authorized the release of the children of Israel. Each time, however, his change of heart was short-lived.

This conflict over authority continued until God spoke His final word regarding the power of Egypt's gods, including that of Pharaoh himself, who was considered a god on the earth. At that point in the battle, a plague of death killed the firstborn in every home that did not have the mark of blood on its lintel and two doorposts—a sign of agreement with God that He would pass over the home and not allow the destroyer in. God demonstrated with a decisive action that His name was the highest authority and power of all (see Exodus 1–12).

Although the children of Israel were miraculously led out of slavery by the hand of God, it did not take them long to question the God they served. While Moses was on Mount Sinai meeting with God and receiving His instructions, the people grew restless. Forty days passed and the people were uncertain of Moses' fate—so they persuaded Aaron to make a god fashioned as a golden calf to worship. They had quickly forgotten their identity in the Lord.

Sin always carries a consequence. On that day three thousand men died. "But where sin abounded, grace abounded much more" (Romans 5:20). In His grace and mercy, God later turned to Aaron and his sons and instructed them to bless the people of Israel with these words:

> "The LORD bless you and keep you;
> The LORD make His face shine upon you,
> And be gracious to you;
> The LORD lift up His countenance upon you,
> And give you peace."
>
> Numbers 6:24–26

The next verse is key: "So they shall put My name on the children of Israel, and I will bless them" (Numbers 6:27). *Put My name.* These words are powerful! As priests appointed by God, Aaron and his sons spoke the words to put God's name on the people, then God released the blessing—a blessing that carried purpose and power.

How does this concept hold power? The Hebraic word for *put* used in this verse is *suwm*, and it has multiple meanings and uses. It conveys authority to "commit, mark, ordain or preserve." In English the word means "to apply, assign, attach, send, start in motion." Using these definitions for *put*, an expanded picture begins to emerge of the power this verse describes:

> "So they shall *commit* My name on the children of Israel, and I will bless them."

> "So they shall *mark* My name on the children of Israel, and I will bless them."

> "So they shall *preserve* My name on the children of Israel, and I will bless them."

> "So they shall *attach* My name on the children of Israel, and I will bless them."

The Lord spoke to Moses and said,

> "If you diligently heed the voice of the LORD your God and do what is right in His sight, give ear to His commandments and keep all His statutes, *I will put* none of the diseases on you which I have brought on the Egyptians. For I am the LORD who heals you."
>
> Exodus 15:26, emphasis added

In the same way that God used the word *put* to speak of placing His name on the children of Israel, He promised that He would not put disease on them as they obeyed His commands. Just as a disease permeates the body, God's name permeates the entire being—body, soul and spirit.

What is in a name? In this case, everything! The name of God carries His presence and permeates with His power to save, His power to protect, His power to deliver, His power to provide, His power to heal and His power to bring complete peace.

Aaron may have been the first priest charged with the responsibility to release God's name, but the priesthood did not end there: "But you are a chosen generation, *a royal priesthood*, a holy nation, His own special people, that you may proclaim the praises of Him who called you out of darkness into His marvelous light" (1 Peter 2:9, emphasis added). As one who has been called into His marvelous light, you have been given priestly authority, responsibility and power to put His name into action to defeat the works of darkness.

What could be better than that?

Pray to Release
the Presence of God

"The LORD Is There"

YAHWEH SHAMMAH

"And the name of the city from that day shall be:
THE LORD IS THERE."

Ezekiel 48:35

From the beginning of time, the presence of the Lord has
infused the earth. The Spirit of God hovered over "the face
of the waters" (Genesis 1:2), and His Spirit hovers over mankind still (see Acts 1:8). In the Garden of Eden, the Lord
God walked in the cool of the day to meet with Adam and

Eve (see Genesis 3:8). Now, where two or three are gathered in the name of Jesus, He is there in the midst of them (see Matthew 18:20).

The final name and title of God revealed in the Old Testament is announced in the last verse of Ezekiel: *Yahweh Shammah*, "The LORD Is There." This name reveals God's nature through His presence and His power. While this title was given as a new name for Jerusalem as it one day will be—a city that will be infused with God's manifest presence, power and glory—this prophetic declaration also points to Jesus the Messiah as He is now, the One who carries the fullness of God through His name *Immanuel*, "God with Us" (see Matthew 1:23).

The Power of the Presence of God

Moses knew the powerful presence of God through personal experience. He first encountered God's presence at the burning bush, when the Lord appeared to him in a flame of fire and revealed Himself by His name I AM (see Exodus 3:2, 14). In the wilderness, God's presence went before Moses and the children of Israel in a pillar of cloud by day and a pillar of fire by night (see Exodus 13:21). After he had spent time in the presence of God on Mount Sinai, Moses' face shone so brightly that it had to be covered with a veil, because the people were afraid to come near him (see Exodus 34:29–35). God's presence was so important that Moses refused to continue leading the people without it, because it was God's presence that set His people apart and made them distinct from all other nations (see Exodus 33:11–16).

Yes, it is the power of God's presence that makes clear who belongs to Him! This power was revealed in Daniel 3, when the presence of God showed up in such an unusual way that even those who worshiped idols were amazed and turned their hearts to worship the living God. Set in ancient Babylon—modern-day Iraq—the king made an image of gold for everyone to worship. It was not a suggestion but a command. For three Jewish exiles living in Babylon, this was not a command they were willing to obey—and their sentence was to be thrown into a fiery furnace.

Their faith in God was mocked. "Who is the god who will deliver you from my hands?" the king challenged.

Unfazed, the men replied, "Our God whom we serve is able to deliver us from the burning fiery furnace, and He will deliver us from your hand, O king" (Daniel 3:17). The men aligned themselves with God, both with their words and with their actions. As they were bound and thrown into the furnace, the flames killed the guards who threw them in. The heat from the furnace was that intense.

As the king watched the scene unfold, he could not believe his eyes. Three men had been thrown into the furnace bound, yet four men could now be seen walking in the fire unharmed, and "the form of the fourth is like the Son of God" (verse 25). When the three men were called to come out of the furnace, it was observed that the fire had had no power over their bodies—their clothes were intact, no smell of the fire could be detected on them and not even a hair on their heads had been singed. Wow! The power of God revealed clearly who belonged to Him, for He was present with them in the flames.

How fitting are these words of God as revealed to Isaiah the prophet, words that these Jewish exiles may well have read and known: "When you pass through the waters, I will be with you; and through the rivers, they shall not overwhelm you; when you walk through fire you shall not be burned, and the flame will not consume you" (Isaiah 43:2 ESV).

Whenever someone is confronted with the power of God's presence, the result is a heightened awareness of God, whether the person believes in Him or not. This awareness frees people to see Him, to hear Him, to discern Him, to know Him. As with Saul on the road to Damascus (see Acts 9), an encounter with God leaves a person forever changed. His presence was powerful to save and deliver then, just as His presence is powerful to save and deliver *now*.

How does God's presence show up today? In what ways is God making Himself known in the Middle East to demonstrate His power? He works through love, because He *is* love. And one of God's love languages is highly visual and impacting—the use of dreams and visions.

"You're killing My people," the ISIS jihadist heard in his dream. Standing before him was a vision of a Man dressed in white. He knew it was Jesus. The fighter who enjoyed killing Christians began to feel uneasy about what he was doing. Later, just before the jihadist committed yet another murder, the Christian who was about to die offered the fighter his own Bible. The fighter killed the Christian, took his Bible . . . and read it.

Love that pursues the one who is lost came after the fighter again. In another dream during the night, Jesus appeared and asked this hardened jihadist to follow Him. Darkness was crushed by the Light, as the fighter turned his heart to the Lord.[1]

Dreams and visions are powerful tools to break through the darkness in the Muslim world, because it is a language many Muslim people understand and respect. It is an acceptable way for them to hear from God because they have the expectation that dreams bring truth. They are especially attentive if a prophet appears to them in a dream—and Jesus is a prophet the Muslim people respect.

Pray that God—*Yahweh Shammah*, "The LORD Is There"— will reveal His presence over the Muslim world through dreams and visions. And as many Muslims begin to have encounters with Jesus through this powerful demonstration of love, pray that He will be revealed to them not just as a prophet but in His identity as *Immanuel*, "God with Us."

——————————— PAUSE TO PRAY ———————————

Lord, I thank You that You are good, and that Your mercy endures forever. I praise You that You do not want anyone to perish but desire that everyone will come to know Your love and repent of his or her sins. Through Jesus, You came to seek and save the lost.

Because You are good and Your goodness overcomes evil, I ask that You increase awareness of Your presence and release Your Spirit in power to give dreams and visions of Jesus to every person in the Middle East who needs a revelation of Him. May Your Spirit hover over them and reveal Jesus as He is—God in the flesh, "God with Us." And may this revelation of Your Son bring light to the darkness, changing hearts and transforming lives.

In the powerful name of Jesus, "The LORD Is There," I pray this in agreement with Your will in faith. Amen!

As you begin to release the purposes of God over the Middle East with prayers targeting specific areas of need, you might be wondering if your prayers will have a tangible effect on the lives of people you do not even know who are so far away. If that is you, be encouraged! Know that you are pressing into the power of God. As you do, the first strategy of the enemy is to fill you with doubt that your prayers will have any effect. The lie that began in the Garden is being spoken to you now: *"Did God actually say . . . ?"* Do you recognize this voice? Whom will you choose to believe? You determine how much power the enemy has in each situation by your words and the agreements you make with him.

Either God wants you to remain in a condition of hopelessness and despair, or He doesn't. Either He has given you a remedy through the power of prayer, or He hasn't. It is clear in His Word what He desires about this. The choice is up to you. So if you are struggling to believe that your prayers have the power to effect change, realize that this is a God-given opportunity for your faith to expand and grow!

Hebrews 11:1 says that faith is "the evidence of things not seen." Faith does not originate with what you see in the natural realm. Great faith is the confident expectation that God will act, even if it cannot be confirmed by what you see or feel. When you call on God in faith, you can expect His answer.

As you release your prayers in faith, ask God for tangible evidence that your prayers are effective. He might direct your attention to a news story or a video report that highlights an answer to the very situation you have been covering in prayer. He might even give you a dream or vision to confirm that your prayer has been answered or as direction for how to pray more specifically still.

What if . . . ? You never learn on this side of heaven the impact your prayers have made. Will that keep you from praying now? Will your faith continue to grow in the presence of opposition? *Will you love Him still?* How you respond to God in this situation is crucial, because He cares about the attitude of your heart. Without faith, it is *impossible* to please Him.

Keep on praying. Press in!

The Promise of the Presence of God

When Jesus lived on the earth, He was pretty impressive by anyone's standards. He healed the sick, restored the lame, gave sight to the blind and hearing to the deaf, cast out demons and raised the dead. He turned water into wine, satisfied the hunger of five thousand people with just five loaves of bread and two fish, walked on water, calmed the raging seas with His words and rose bodily from the dead.

Even more amazing is that Jesus said that whoever believes in Him will do greater works than these: "Most assuredly, I say to you, he who believes in Me, the works that I do he will do also; and greater works than these he will do, because I go to My Father" (John 14:12). *Greater works!* How is that even possible? The answer lies in the responsibility of the believer and in the promise of the Father.

Greater works begin with belief. Faith in Jesus releases His power to work. Scripture records an instance in which Jesus was unable to do mighty works—"except that He laid His hands on a few sick people and healed them"—because of unbelief in the hearts of the people (see Mark 6:5). And this was in His own hometown! If you want to walk in His footsteps, you must do your part and *believe.*

It is in the promise of the Father that the power to do as Jesus did is released to the one who believes. Following His resurrection, Jesus instructed His disciples to wait for the promise of the Father, which would give them the power they needed to preach repentance and forgiveness of sins to all the nations (see Luke 24:47–49).

What is the promise of the Father? It is the infilling presence of the Holy Spirit: "You shall receive power when the Holy Spirit has come upon you" (Acts 1:8). When God pours out His Spirit, incredible things happen. Prophecies, dreams, visions, healings, miracles, signs, wonders, salvations, deliverances, tongues to speak in other languages the mighty works of God—all of these (and more!) result when the powerful presence of God has been released.

God's name "The LORD Is There" connects Him to the promise of His presence. "For no matter how many promises God has made, they are 'Yes' in Christ. And so through him *the 'Amen' is spoken by us* to the glory of God" (2 Corinthians 1:20 NIV, emphasis added). God speaks the promise, Jesus answers, "Yes," and your voice is the "Amen," setting into motion the purposes of God. What a beautiful picture of the harmony found through agreement with God's promises! Your "Amen" is your agreement with God's Word, your declaration that gives Him the glory—a statement of faith wrapped up in one powerful word that means "Let it be so!"

Here are key verses of promise for you to hold on to in agreement with His promise:

"And He said, 'My Presence will go with you, and I will give you rest'" (Exodus 33:14). *Amen!*

"For He Himself has said, 'I will never leave you nor forsake you'" (Hebrews 13:5). *Amen!*

"And lo, I am with you always, even to the end of the age" (Matthew 28:20). *Amen!*

In the presence of darkness, light shines brighter still. Believers in the Middle East who are surrounded by the cruelty of ISIS need to be comforted and strengthened by the powerful presence of God that dwells in them. Pray that the presence of the Holy Spirit will fill them with courage, and that the promise of His presence will result in greater awareness of His Spirit at all times, releasing hope in their hearts as their faith continues to expand and grow.

—————————————— PAUSE TO PRAY ——————————————

Lord, I thank You that You are faithful to Your Word and to Your promises. I praise You that times of refreshing come while in Your presence.

Bring the comforting presence of Your Holy Spirit now to my brothers and sisters in the Middle East, filling them with courage as their awareness of Your nearness is taken to new heights. Release Your hope into their hearts—hope that does not disappoint, as their faith in You expands to grow deeper and stronger. As Your presence increases, may they do the greater works Jesus promised they would do, as You work healings, deliverances, miracles, signs and wonders through their hands, for Your name's sake and for Your glory.

In the powerful name of Jesus, "The LORD Is There," I pray this in agreement with Your will in faith. Amen!

Pray to Release the Presence of God

There is a community of believers in Baghdad, Iraq, who take enormous risks as they gather to worship each week. Surrounded by blast walls and protected by armed guards in battle fatigues carrying AK-47s, St. George's Church is located in the "Red Zone"—an unstable area of Baghdad and one of the most dangerous areas of the city. The people must pass through rigorous security checks before they are allowed inside. Precautions are necessary as the church has suffered multiple bombings, and through the years many of the people have been kidnapped and killed for their faith. All have experienced loss.

Yet in times of greatest suffering, the believers of St. George's have experienced God's presence in powerful and tangible ways. In the midst of their tragedy, God is real and present with them. "We only knew Jesus was all we needed when He was all we had left," said Canon Andrew White, the British clergyman who re-opened the church in 1998, but who since was forced to leave the country when ISIS invaded Iraq.[2]

It is not surprising that the presence of God is actively released over the congregation at St. George's. For years, Canon White would begin each worship service with these words spoken in Aramaic, the language of Jesus: "The LORD is here and His Spirit is with us." A prophetic declaration that placed the name of God, *Yahweh Shammah*, over the people and over the place they met to worship. A prophetic declaration that invited a response—and agreement in faith that was answered by the Holy One, the great I AM.

This is the reason prayer to release God's presence is so important. God is not powerless to act, but He waits on you to join your voice with His in agreement through declaration and prayer for His Kingdom to come and His will to be done on earth as it is in heaven. "Oh, that You would rend the heavens! That You would come down! That the mountains might shake at Your presence . . . to make Your name known to Your adversaries, that the nations may tremble at Your presence!" (Isaiah 64:1–2).

Pray for His Kingdom—His rule, His presence and His power—to come into this situation in the Middle East now.

PAUSE TO PRAY

Lord, I thank You that in Your presence there is fullness of joy. I praise You that Your presence sets Your people apart as the infilling of Your Holy Spirit releases Your power and identifies those who belong to You.

Come now and hover over Your people in the Middle East, making Yourself known in a fresh new way as "The Lord Is There" and as "God with Us." Expand the ability of Your people to see You, to hear You, to sense You, to know You as You bring them into the comfort of Your presence. As darkness in this region grows stronger, may Your light in Your people grow brighter still, until Your light overcomes the darkness.

Strengthen Your people to remain in Your presence so that they will not give in to desperation or fear—for You are the One who lifts their heads so they can keep their focus on Jesus. Remind them of Your promise never to leave them or forsake them, as You are with them to the end of the age.

Make Your name and Your presence known to the people who have yet to call on You, confronting them with Your love that goes after the lost. May Your Kingdom come and Your will be done in the Middle East, just as it is done in heaven.

In the powerful name of Jesus, "The LORD *Is There," I pray this in agreement with Your will in faith. Amen!*

As you pray this prayer in faith, you join your voice with mine in agreement for the Father's will to be done. Jesus said, "Again I say to you that if two of you agree on earth concerning anything that they ask, it will be done for them by My Father in heaven" (Matthew 18:19). These are radical words! Let your faith rise up to match these words with great expectation for what the Lord will do.

As you pray through these prayer strategies, I invite you to keep your Bible and a journal next to you. Wait on the Lord and ask Him if there is anything more He desires to release to you. He might direct your attention to another verse or passage, or He might speak to your spirit in His still, small voice. Wait on Him and listen. Write down what you hear Him speak. You will be blessed if you do, as wisdom comes to those who seek Him (see Proverbs 3:13 ESV).

Pray to Release
the Armies of God

"The LORD of Hosts"

YAHWEH TZEVA'OT

As for our Redeemer, the LORD of hosts is His name,
the Holy One of Israel.

Isaiah 47:4

Military Strategist. Supreme Power. Universal Ruler. All of
these inherent attributes give descriptive insight into the
powerful name of God as revealed to all creation: *Yahweh
Tzeva'ot*, "The LORD of Hosts."

What is a host? When used as a title of God, this word
typically brings to mind an image of the heavenly beings who

suddenly appeared to the shepherds at night as an angel announced the birth of Jesus. A host, however, is much more than that. In Hebrew the primary meaning of the word *tzeva* is "army." That is powerful! This word can refer to a company of angels or people organized for war, to celestial bodies such as the sun, moon and stars, or to the whole of creation. "The Lord of Hosts" is the Lord of all.

The zeal of "The Lord of Hosts" would bring forth the Messiah, as described in a beautiful, prophetic passage found in Isaiah 9:6–7:

> For unto us a Child is born, unto us a Son is given; and the government will be upon His shoulder. And His name will be called Wonderful, Counselor, Mighty God, Everlasting Father, Prince of Peace. Of the increase of His government and peace there will be no end. . . . The zeal of the Lord of hosts will perform this.

Onto the shoulders of His Son, Jesus, "The Lord of Hosts" places authority and power so that He may rule and reign: Military Strategist, Supreme Power, Universal Ruler . . . *Lord of all.*

Military Strategist

Goliath had a strategy. It was quite simple, actually. Be bigger, taller and stronger than any enemy soldier who dares to fight, and you will win. Standing tall at 9 feet 9 inches and weighing more than six hundred pounds, it was a strategy that served him well.

For forty days, each morning and evening, Goliath came down the hill from the Philistine camp dressed in full body armor to taunt the armies of Israel. His armor alone weighed

175 pounds—just the sight of him was enough to strike fear in the hearts of his opponents and cause them to flee.

"Choose a man and have him come down to me. If he is able to fight and kill me, we will become your subjects; but if I overcome him and kill him, you will become our subjects and serve us" (1 Samuel 17:8–9 NIV). No one dared to take Goliath up on his challenge.

Until one day when a shepherd boy entered the battle scene with a strategy that trumped the giant's.

With no armor to protect him and no military weapon to depend on, David drew near and faced the Philistine with supreme confidence in the strategy given him by the Spirit of God: Victory would come *in the name* of "The LORD of Hosts." Though Goliath thought it beneath him to fight an opponent so seemingly insignificant, David was his fiercest foe: Fearless and full of faith, David had chosen the God of angel armies to be at his side:

> "You come to me with a sword, with a spear, and with a javelin. But I come to you in the name of the LORD of hosts, the God of the armies of Israel, whom you have defied. This day the LORD will deliver you into my hand, and I will strike you and take your head from you."
>
> 1 Samuel 17:45–46

The Holy Spirit reveals the strategies of God to the hearts of those who are yielded to Him. With these strategies, He releases prophetic declarations of His purposes. Rather than focus on the obstacles in front of him, David kept his eyes on God and made a prophetic declaration in faith. He declared to Goliath not only that he would kill him, but that the armies of the Philistines who had gathered against Israel would also perish in the fight. And it happened just as he said (see 1 Samuel 17). David's declarations released the purposes of God and the destiny He had prepared.

Strategy and declarations work hand in hand.

ISIS has a strategy, too. It is closely related to the strategy Goliath used because it relies on the perception of strength. To the outcast wanting to belong and seeking a sense of purpose, it calls out, "Come to the Islamic State and be part of something important." To the onlooking world, it intimidates through psychological warfare by flaunting its cruelty and celebrating its atrocities, attempting to establish a state of terror—for in that state, its enemies are rendered helpless as they accept defeat.

It was the perception of Goliath's strength that caused the armies of Israel to lose the will to fight, just as it was the perception of ISIS's strength that caused the Iraqi soldiers to lay down their weapons and flee at the first sight of jihadists entering Mosul.

This perception the weak have of their opponent's strength—whether their fears are founded or not—further emboldens their foe.

To implement its strategy, ISIS has relied on a jihadist text written in 2004 called "The Management of Savagery." The tactics used to achieve domination are outlined in three phases: (1) Disruption and Exhaustion—damage the economy and demoralize the population; (2) Management of Savagery— carry out highly visible acts of violence, sending a message to both allies and enemies; and (3) Empowerment—establish regions controlled by jihadists that can grow and unite into the re-creation of a caliphate.[1] Following closely to the script and just nineteen days following the takeover of Mosul in 2014, ISIS made its bold declaration: "The caliphate is established!"

This enemy recognizes the strength of declarations. It is the power of agreement in action once again—a transfer of authority by ISIS to the power of darkness. Just ten years had elapsed since the jihadist text was first made public, and ISIS was clearly able to meet these strategic objectives. The effects of ISIS's strategy have already been far-reaching.

Frequent and prolonged exposure to savagery reduces a person's capacity to feel empathy for another, fueling the fire for jihadists to participate in further acts of violence and extreme cruelty. War crimes against children have created an army of fighters for whom violence is an accepted way of life, as ISIS uses indoctrination tactics, beatings and terror against its youngest victims to establish lifelong loyalty.

Most effective of all, however, has been ISIS's social media strategy to extend its influence into homes around the globe, distributing sophisticated videos and media messages in an attempt to alter perception and transform attitudes— propaganda techniques designed to entice both seasoned fighters and recruits to violent extremes, while demoralizing and debilitating those they set to conquer.

So that is the bad news—the *really* bad news. Are you ready for the good?

The act of pulling down strongholds begins as ISIS's strategy is revealed. Light shines to expose the works of darkness (see Ephesians 5:11–14). As important as it is to know your enemy, it is even more important to understand the power at work *within you* by "The Lord of Hosts": "For the weapons of our warfare are not carnal but mighty in God for pulling down strongholds" (2 Corinthians 10:4). As a believer in Jesus, you have the mind of Christ (see 1 Corinthians 2:16). God promises wisdom to those who ask in faith (see James 1:5–6).

Take encouragement in these words from Solomon, the king who asked for wisdom above anything else that God could offer: "Wisdom is better than weapons of war" (Ecclesiastes 9:18).

PAUSE TO PRAY

Lord, I thank You that through the power of Your Holy Spirit, You release strategies to overcome darkness and evil. I praise You that the ultimate victory over darkness and death has already been won at the cross through the obedience of Your Son. Thank You that You have given me weapons of warfare that are mighty in You to demolish every stronghold of the enemy and to tear down every argument that is in opposition to You. Release Your wisdom to me now.

Break the power of darkness and evil as I speak Your truth in prayer. Halt the advance of ISIS and cause the enemy to scatter. Expose every lie that Satan has spoken into each heart and mind. Reveal the darkness of this deception to ISIS fighters and sympathizers—darkness that keeps them captive in a prison of hate. Remove these blinders as You shine Your light of truth into the darkest of hearts—truth that declares the name of Jesus above every name now and every name that is to come. And by His name, I declare the victory over ISIS is Yours!

In the powerful name of Jesus, "The LORD of Hosts," I pray this in agreement with Your will in faith. Amen!

Goliath approached David with three weapons of warfare—a sword, a spear and a javelin. The sword was used for cutting and was a symbol of honor and authority. The spear was used as a thrusting weapon at close range. The javelin was a light spear thrown at targets at a distance. Both spear and javelin were symbols of power. Goliath's weapons were carnal.

But David came clothed in the name of "The LORD of Hosts." Honor, authority and power are not just symbolic of His name but the essential fabric of His nature. David's weapon was eternal.

David's weapon won the victory.

It takes only one David to defeat a Goliath. Are you ready to be that one David with your prayers?

Supreme Power

The strategy meetings took place in secret, in the bedroom of a king. Certainly that was a safe and private place to develop plans for a military invasion. It is too bad the king in question was plotting an invasion against the king of Israel, though, who had "The LORD of Hosts" on his side. No such plans are kept hidden from His sight.

God revealed to His servant Elisha the words that the king of Syria spoke in secret as he plotted against Israel—a scene that played out more than once or twice. And on each occasion, Elisha was able to warn the king of Israel and avert disaster. This exasperated and enraged the Syrian king into action. He ordered his men to find Elisha and to seize him.

During the night a great army of soldiers with their horses and chariots surrounded the city where Elisha was sleeping. In the early morning hours, Elisha's servant got up and saw the enemy enclosing them. He panicked. "Oh no, my lord! What shall we do?" (2 Kings 6:15 NIV).

Elisha's faith was strong; his servant's faith was weak.

Full of faith and confidence, Elisha encouraged his servant not to be afraid, "for those who are with us are more than those who are with them" (2 Kings 6:16 ESV). Elisha could see into a spiritual reality that his servant could not. He prayed to "The LORD of Hosts" that the eyes of his servant would be opened.

The opening of his eyes silenced his fears.

With his spiritual eyesight now engaged, the servant saw that the mountain was also filled with horses and chariots of fire. "The LORD of Hosts" had sent His angel armies to protect Elisha and to fight on his behalf.

As the Syrians came down to capture him, Elisha prayed that the Lord would strike them blind. And so He did. Not only did He blind their eyes, but He blinded their minds with confusion as well.

Elisha met his enemy and said, "Follow me, and I will bring you to the man whom you seek" (2 Kings 6:19). The Syrians had Elisha within their grasp and did not even know it. Elisha led the soldiers into Samaria—and into the presence of his king.

Now that he had them where he wanted them, Elisha prayed one more time. "O LORD, open the eyes of these men, that they may see" (2 Kings 6:20 ESV). When their eyes were opened, the Syrians knew that they were in trouble. They saw Elisha's king—and his king wanted them dead.

But Elisha was moved by a different spirit.

Elisha did not bring the soldiers to his king so that they could be killed. His purpose was to bring them into submission to the King of kings, "The LORD of Hosts." Elisha told Israel's king to give their enemies bread and water and send them back to their master. Elisha showed mercy to those who hated him.

Following Elisha's example, the king of Israel did one better—instead of simply giving bread and water, he prepared a feast for his enemies before releasing them. Supreme power is demonstrated in more than just an act of military might. The Supreme Power moved the heart of the king to spare the lives of his enemies—the most powerful act of all. The Syrian army did not come again to raid the land of Israel (see 2 Kings 6:8–23).

This story can be summed up beautifully in the words of the apostle Paul to the believers in Rome:

> Do not take revenge, my dear friends, but leave room for God's wrath, for it is written: "It is mine to avenge; I will repay," says the Lord. On the contrary: "If your enemy is hungry, feed him; if he is thirsty, give him something to drink. In doing this, you will heap burning coals on his head." Do not be overcome by evil, but overcome evil with good.
>
> Romans 12:19–21 NIV

Overcome evil with good. It was great advice then—it is great advice now. That is the power of God at work in you.

PAUSE TO PRAY

Lord, I thank You that You are good and that Your goodness overcomes evil. I praise You that You are a refuge and a strength, an ever-present help in times of trouble. Open the eyes of Your people who are being persecuted by ISIS, that they may see Your power surrounding them as a shield from their enemies. May the opening of their eyes silence their every fear. Give them courage to declare in faith, "Greater is He who is in me than he who is in the world."

You are the One who frustrates the enemy's plans, making wars to cease as Your government and peace increase in power. Send Your angel armies into every region of the Middle East to rout ISIS and sever all its evil schemes. Bring ISIS fighters into the presence of the King as You open their eyes to see You and their ears to hear Your voice. As they are confronted by the Supreme Power, may they lose all will and desire to fight or do evil. I declare that through the greatness of Your power, ISIS fighters will submit themselves to You, Yahweh Tzeva'ot!

In the powerful name of Jesus, "The LORD *of Hosts," I pray this in agreement with Your will in faith. Amen!*

The power of God that transformed lives then continues to transform lives today.

She was appalled to see a beheading. A friend had sent her a link to an ISIS video, created to shock and horrify. In graphic detail, the video showed the decapitation of an American. When she heard the Quran being recited by the jihadist as he did the killing, she was stunned. She was a Muslim, too.

Raised in Somalia, she had recited Arabic prayers throughout her life. Now for the first time, she prayed from her heart.

God, is this really You? Is this what You want? Is this who You are?

That night God answered her in a dream. She had a vision of a glorious figure in white, descending from heaven. Surrounding Him was a multitude of people on the earth, worshiping Him.

She was one of the worshipers.

She knew that this was right and good—that it was the answer she had been seeking to the questions of her heart. She became a believer in Jesus, and her husband joined her in the faith.[2]

What the enemy intended for evil, God used for good. Good that overcame evil. Good that brought a powerful victory from the cross.

Universal Ruler

Declaring the high praises of God, one seraph called to another, "Holy, holy, holy is the LORD of hosts; the whole earth is full of His glory!" (Isaiah 6:3). The sound waves from his voice shook the building to its foundation, as the entire Temple filled with smoke. In this atmosphere of worship, Isaiah saw *Yahweh Tzeva'ot*, "The LORD of Hosts," seated on His throne. It was a vision that left him undone.

The throne of God was exalted, high and lifted up. His throne was above every other throne, revealing His dominion and power over all other powers, both in heaven and on earth (see Psalm 103:19). His throne is the throne of glory, where all bow down in worship (see Revelation 7:11). His throne is the throne of government, where He judges in righteousness (see Psalm 9:4). His throne is the throne of grace, a place where mercy reigns (see Hebrews 4:16).

Isaiah's vision revealed God's holiness. His holiness displays His purity combined with His power. History has shown that power without purity is a terrifying force—a cruel breeding ground for evil. For an example, look no further than ISIS.

God's holiness uncovered Isaiah's sinfulness so that the prophet could be cleansed. With his lips purified from the burning coal of the altar, Isaiah was made ready to speak the word of the Lord and receive his assignment.

Isaiah heard the voice of the Lord saying, "Whom shall I send, and who will go for Us?"

Isaiah was quick to respond. "Here am I! Send me."

And God said, "Go."

God is still looking for people like Isaiah—people prepared with a yes in their hearts to do whatever He asks, whatever the cost (see Isaiah 6:1–9).

These are the armies of the Lord!

Centuries later Isaiah's vision was repeated for John when he was on the island of Patmos—a vision that John recorded in the book of Revelation. John also saw the Lord seated on His throne in heaven, with four living creatures that never ceased to say, "Holy, holy, holy, Lord God Almighty, who was and is and is to come!" (Revelation 4:8; see also 1–11).

Isaiah's writings point to Jesus as deity (see also Isaiah 45:23), and John's revelation affirms it. As the apostle Paul wrote to the Philippians:

> Therefore God also has highly exalted Him and given Him the name which is above every name, that at the name of Jesus every knee should bow, of those in heaven, and of those on earth, and of those under the earth, and that every tongue should confess that Jesus Christ is Lord, to the glory of God the Father.
>
> Philippians 2:9–11

The end of the story is clear. One day every knee will bow to the name of Jesus. It is not a matter of "if" but "when." The One who is love will stand in the face of ISIS for the final victory.

"The LORD of Hosts" is the Lord of all.

Thank You, Lord, that You are righteous and holy. I praise You that You are lifted up and exalted—above all people, nations, rulers and powers. Yahweh Tzeva'ot, there is none like You!

Thank You for extending Your righteousness to me through my faith in Jesus, cleansing me of all my sin. You call me to be holy, as You are holy. Increase my faith to believe Your promises, until great faith rises up and shatters every doubt and thought that does not line up with Yours.

I join with Your armies of believers, boldly releasing Your purposes here on earth through the power of Your name. Where there is darkness, release Your light. Where there is evil, release Your love. Turn those with the hardest of hearts to look on Your face and receive Your mercy while there is still time. Father, forgive. You are that good. Make my heart like Yours.

I declare that all nations of the world will bow in awe and fear of Your name, because the earth is Yours and all it contains belongs to You!

*In the powerful name of Jesus, "The L*ORD* of Hosts," I pray this in agreement with Your will in faith. Amen!*

Light comes to shatter the darkness.

A man with a big beard climbed into the taxi. The cab driver recognized him right away—not because he knew him by name, but because he recognized him by vocation. The

Christian driver had just picked up a Muslim sheik, a religious teacher of Islamic law.

The sheik was on his way to the airport, returning to his home in Saudi Arabia. But he had one unusual request before being dropped off.

"I want to find a Bible," the sheik told his driver. "Can you find me a Bible?"

The taxi driver took the sheik to a Christian worker who was happy to comply with this request. As the sheik received his new Bible, the driver could not help but ask why he wanted a Bible of his own.

The sheik explained that he was returning from Syria, where he had been teaching ISIS fighters about Islam, both its theology and practice. The evil he was exposed to while with the jihadist armies had taken its toll.

His answer was simple.

"I'm sick of the killing," the sheik replied. "There must be something better than this."[3]

"The people dwelling in darkness have seen a great light, and for those dwelling in the region and shadow of death, on them a light has dawned" (Matthew 4:16 ESV).

Pray to Release the Protection of God

"The LORD Is My Shepherd"

YAHWEH RO'I

> The LORD is my shepherd; I shall not want.
>
> Psalm 23:1

Written by a shepherd to the great Shepherd, Psalm 23 is one of the most beloved and quoted passages in the Bible. David begins his song with the introduction of God's name *Yahweh Ro'i*, "The LORD Is My Shepherd." Who better to give illustrative insight into the nature of God as a shepherd than David, who from an early age knew by experience the responsibilities of this role himself?

A shepherd's primary job is to protect the sheep—leading, defending and rescuing the flock while taking care of every need.

It is Jesus who fulfills the role of a shepherd in its entirety. He is the "good shepherd" who lays down His life for the sheep (John 10:11), the "great Shepherd" who was raised from the dead (Hebrews 13:20), and the "Chief Shepherd" who will appear again (1 Peter 5:4).

In times of trouble, the need for the Shepherd's protection is never more acute. Scripture is filled with testimonies of those who cried out to God in their distress, and He answered their prayers—prayers spoken in agreement with His will, prayers that released His response for protection. "In your distress you called and I rescued you" (Psalm 81:7 NIV).

Releasing the Protection of God through Leadership

God spoke to Moses with a command and a grim prophetic word. The command was for Moses to climb a mountainous region in Jordan where he would be able to see the land God had given to the people of Israel. It was there he would die because of his one act of rebellion against God as he led the people through the wilderness (see Numbers 27:12–14). Moses would see the Promised Land, but he would not inherit the promise himself.

God holds leaders to a very high standard.

Rather than argue with God or beg for mercy, Moses accepted his fate and asked God to appoint another leader in his place after his death.

"Let the LORD, the God of the spirits of all flesh, appoint a man over the congregation who shall go out before them and come in before them, who shall lead them out and bring them in, that the congregation of the LORD may not be as sheep that have no shepherd."

Numbers 27:16–17 ESV

Moses embraced his role of leadership like a shepherd (see Psalm 77:20). He had been a shepherd for forty years for his father-in-law, Jethro, when he lived in Midian. It was while guarding the flock, with his shepherd's staff in hand, that he encountered God in the burning bush (see Exodus 3; 4:2 NLT). Moses spent the next forty years shepherding the people of Israel out of captivity and into freedom.

Through Moses' leadership in his role as a shepherd, the protection of God was released over the people.

This was providential, because the people of Israel had a tendency to scatter like sheep without a shepherd. It did not take long. Early in their journey, while Moses was on Mount Sinai for forty days receiving the commandments of God, they turned away from God to worship the golden calf they had made. As their leader, Moses interceded for the people to be spared from death. God listened to Moses and relented from bringing disaster, releasing His protection in the face of certain tragedy (see Exodus 32:11–14).

The metaphor of a shepherd is used in Scripture to refer to kings, princes and religious leaders—those who hold authority (see Psalm 78:70–72; Jeremiah 23:2). The apostle Paul speaks to believers in 1 Timothy 2:1–4 to encourage prayer and intercession for leaders and all those who are in authority. This prayer is good and is "pleasing in the sight of God our Savior, who desires all people to be saved and to come to the knowledge of the truth" (verses 3–4 ESV).

When Paul wrote this prayer directive, the governing authorities were enemies of Christianity and persecutors of Christians. Paul had been beaten and imprisoned many times by leaders such as these. Yet he said not only to intercede for them but to give thanks for them.

This is perhaps the most difficult instruction of all in this passage. Is it really possible to give thanks for those who are enemies of the cross? From a human perspective, the answer is clearly no.

But God is calling His children to pray into the situation in the Middle East from heaven's perspective: "Since you have been raised to new life with Christ, set your sights on the realities of heaven, where Christ sits in the place of honor at God's right hand" (Colossians 3:1 NLT). The realities of heaven are at times vastly different from the realities experienced on earth.

Paul showed by example that giving thanks for leaders can be accomplished through the supernatural infilling of the Holy Spirit. In this he carried out Jesus' command to "love your enemies, bless those who curse you, do good to those who hate you, and pray for those who spitefully use you and persecute you, that you may be sons of your Father in heaven" (Matthew 5:44–45).

How do you pray for leaders in the Middle East conflict? First, pray that all leaders will be saved and come to the knowledge of the truth. Pray that leaders will be confronted with God's holiness and pursue peace (see Hebrews 12:14) as hearts are turned to Him (see Proverbs 21:1).

Next, pray that God will release His wisdom, and that godly discernment will rule in every decision that is made (see Proverbs 2:2–5). Pray that leaders will govern with justice and righteousness (see 1 Kings 10:9). Pray that leaders will have insight to see beyond the immediate needs and concerns facing them, and that they will protect and cover future generations with their decisions (see Isaiah 39).

Finally, pray for the pastors and leaders who are caring for the people of God. Pray that God will guard them as they protect their flocks through the leadership principles God has set in place for shepherds (see Ezekiel 34:2–4).

PAUSE TO PRAY

Thank You, Lord, that You have given me the privilege of praying for the leaders in the Middle East. I praise You that You give Your wisdom when I ask. Yahweh Ro'i, *lead me now in wisdom as I pray with my spirit and with understanding.*

Thank You for the governmental leaders You have set in place in the nations of the Middle East. Confront them with Your holiness, opening their eyes to see You as You are. Turn their hearts to You, that they may come to the saving knowledge of Jesus as their Messiah. Expose the leaders who are set on doing evil and remove them from their positions of power. In their places, appoint leaders whose hope and trust is in You.

Release Your wisdom so that leaders will rule with godly discernment. May they be ones who pursue peace—peace with God and peace with mankind. Give them hearts to govern their nations with justice and righteousness. Give them vision to see beyond the troubles that face them today, helping them to make wise decisions that will benefit both present and future generations.

Protect the pastors and leaders who are shepherding Your people in the Middle East. Draw near to them as they lead others with gentleness into deeper levels of faith and trust in You. Give them wisdom and understanding as they set an example by walking in love, mercy and forgiveness. May they hear Your voice more clearly than ever before as they saturate themselves in Your Word and in Your presence. Empower them to strengthen the weak, heal the sick, bind up the broken, bring back what was driven away and seek out the lost.

In the powerful name of Jesus, "The LORD Is My Shepherd," *I pray this in agreement with Your will in faith. Amen!*

Scripture gives many examples of God's protection being released through leadership. When Pharaoh finally gave permission for Moses and the Israelites to leave Egypt, God directed them around the wilderness and away from their enemies (see Exodus 13:17–18). God protected the people as He led them with a pillar of cloud by day and a pillar of fire by night (see Exodus 13:21–22).

In the Psalms David often speaks of being led and upheld by God's right hand (see Psalm 139:10). David said, "I will cry to You, when my heart is overwhelmed; lead me to the rock that is higher than I. For You have been a shelter for me, a strong tower from the enemy" (Psalm 61:2–3).

Jesus told His disciples that He would ask the Father to give another Advocate who would never leave them—"He is the Holy Spirit, who leads into all truth" (John 14:16–17

NLT). Physical and spiritual protection is released through the leadership of the Holy Spirit.

The Holy Spirit descended on Jesus at His baptism (see Luke 3:21–22), led Jesus into the wilderness for a time of testing (see Luke 4:1), and empowered Jesus when He returned to the Galilee region for ministry (see Luke 4:14). The power of the Holy Spirit then provided physical protection by enabling Jesus to walk unharmed through crowds attempting to throw Him over a cliff (see Luke 4:28–30), and His power now provides spiritual protection through the sword of the Spirit, which is the Word of God (see Ephesians 6:17).

The ultimate protection given through the leadership of the Shepherd will be evident one day when those who come out of the Great Tribulation are standing before the throne of God.

> "He who sits on the throne will give them shelter. They will never again be hungry or thirsty; they will never be scorched by the heat of the sun. For the Lamb on the throne will be their Shepherd. He will lead them to springs of life-giving water. And God will wipe every tear from their eyes."
>
> Revelation 7:15–17 NLT

Releasing the Protection of God through Defense

She was awakened at two a.m. by cars driving past her home, blaring a message on loudspeakers for all the Christians to hear: "Pay the *jizya*, convert to Islam, be killed or leave." ISIS had come to her neighborhood, and she was terrified.

She was not ignorant of their presence. A month earlier, a mass exodus of Christians had occurred when ISIS first arrived in Mosul—but she and her family chose to remain behind. Her husband had encountered ISIS fighters on the streets who told him, "Don't be afraid. We're not here for you." She believed they were safe.

Now she knew differently. She went with her husband to ask about the religious tax. It was then she learned there was no option about paying the *jizya*—ISIS had lied. The couple had three daughters, ages eighteen, seventeen and eleven. They had little choice but to leave.

Clinging to their faith in Jesus, Shatha and her husband abandoned their home, their car and their workshop that provided their livelihood. She gave her daughters the traditional Muslim *hijab* (veil) and long clothing to wear to conceal their identities. They left Mosul with just the clothes on their backs and the few possessions they could carry.

Her Muslim neighbors, close friends, gathered Shatha, her husband, her brother and her daughters into their car to drive them to safety. They headed for Qaraqosh, a predominantly Christian town just thirty minutes away.

They did not get far. Along the way, ISIS stopped their car and questioned their driver. Shatha's husband and brother were taken to a caravan of ISIS vehicles. Shatha was convinced she would never see them alive again. She prayed to God that her daughters would be spared from harm.

"The LORD Is My Shepherd" heard Shatha's prayer.

Not only were her daughters miraculously spared, but ten minutes later her husband and brother were set free. With their money, cell phones, medicines and personal belongings confiscated, Shatha's family began to walk toward the nearest town.

They found refuge in Qaraqosh, where a group of Syrian Catholics from the local seminary welcomed them into their homes, providing food, clothing and shelter. Their stay was short-lived. Just fifteen days later, ISIS came storming into

Qaraqosh, and Shatha's family was displaced once again. They fled to Erbil, where they stayed in temporary camps set up by Christians until visas were made available for the family to live as refugees in Jordan.

"In my desperation I prayed, and the LORD listened; he saved me from all my troubles. For the angel of the LORD is a guard; he surrounds and defends all who fear him" (Psalm 34:6–7 NLT). Throughout their terrifying experience, Shatha prayed constantly to the Lord for His help. She and her family experienced the reality of this psalm of David, as God released His protection over them during every step of their journey.

The presence of God surrounded them to protect them from physical harm—and His presence surrounded them to defend their faith in Jesus.

Protection and defense work in harmony to release the purposes of God as *Yahweh Ro'i*. Isaiah spoke prophetically to King Hezekiah as he shared the word of the Lord regarding God's purposes for the fate of Jerusalem: "For my own honor and for the sake of my servant David, I will defend this city and protect it" (2 Kings 19:34 NLT). He is the defender of the widow, the orphan and the poor (see Deuteronomy 10:18; Psalm 68:5; Proverbs 22:23), and He is the protector of His people: "The LORD is my fortress, protecting me from danger" (Psalm 27:1 NLT).

There is ongoing need for the protection and defense of religious minority groups impacted by ISIS's presence in the Middle East. ISIS continues to overtake towns and villages as it seeks to extend its caliphate, targeting Christians that remain in the region.[1] Regarding them as infidels, ISIS abducts these men, women and children to be used as human shields.[2] Younger women and girls—some as young as eight years old—are forced into the sex slave trade to be offered first to

ISIS leaders, followed by ISIS fighters, with the remainder auctioned off to the highest bidder.[3] Many are bought and sold numerous times, as they are traded from one terrorist to another.[4]

PAUSE TO PRAY

Lord, thank You for being Yahweh Ro'i, *protector and defender of the weak. I praise You that You are the God of justice and righteousness.*

May Your fierce protection be released over every person ISIS has targeted with evil intentions, as You defend the innocent with Your fiery passion for justice. Surround them with Your angels to shield them and guard them from harm. May all persons who are oppressed and persecuted know You intimately as "The Lord Is My Shepherd"—*the One who is present with them in valleys of deepest darkness and the One who restores their souls. May Your authority be their strength and their peace as the comfort of Your love takes away all their fear.*

Break the power of ISIS as You call each fighter to account personally for every act of evil. Bring an end to the jihadists' violence as You show them Your eagerness to defend Your people. You will not be mocked. You say that "the violence of the wicked will destroy them, because they refuse to do justice" *(Proverbs 21:7). Destroy ISIS. Let Your justice prevail. I declare that nothing is too difficult for You!*

In the powerful name of Jesus, "The Lord Is My Shepherd," *I pray this in agreement with Your will in faith. Amen!*

Releasing the Protection of God through Rescue

In one memorable parable spoken to the tax collectors, sinners, Pharisees and scribes, Jesus portrays a shepherd as one who rescues, demonstrating the care of God to go after the one in need of help.

> "If a man has a hundred sheep and one of them gets lost, what will he do? Won't he leave the ninety-nine others in the wilderness and go to search for the one that is lost until he finds it? And when he has found it, he will joyfully carry it home on his shoulders."
>
> Luke 15:4–5 NLT

The Shepherd's focus is intense. He is relentless in His pursuit until the lost is carried home on His shoulders. What a beautiful picture of love!

"My heart was dark," Zaki confessed to me on a rooftop overlooking a city in Jordan. "I forgot my Lord. I didn't open my heart for Him. It was so dirty."

Zaki had lived in the city of Qaraqosh, Iraq, with his wife and two children. He worked as a teacher and owned a shop selling mobile phones and computers. Zaki knew Jesus as his Savior but did not make time for Him. His work and the daily activities of life kept him busy enough.

When the Christians who were forced out of Mosul streamed into his city in June 2014, they came with nothing. Zaki joined in to help. Everything that the displaced people needed—food, clothing, places to live, even air conditioners and refrigerators—was provided as the Christians of Qaraqosh opened their doors and welcomed them in.

It never crossed Zaki's mind that he could face a similar fate. One day soon, the rescuer would need rescuing.

Zaki believed his situation was different from those who had lived in Mosul. The leader of Kurdistan had promised that the *peshmerga* (Kurdish military forces) would stay to protect the Christians of Qaraqosh. Thus far the military had been able to prevent ISIS from entering the city. The people felt safe.

At midnight on August 6, 2014, the church bells in Qaraqosh began to ring. Something was very wrong.

Zaki learned quickly that the Kurdish fighters had deserted the city, retreating to Erbil when ISIS broke through their ranks. Zaki took one bag of clothes, hurried his wife and children into their car, and left.

The usual one-hour drive to Erbil turned into a long and miserable ordeal as Zaki drove through the night on overcrowded roadways, stopping at checkpoints all along the way. Twelve hours later, Zaki and his family arrived in Erbil tired and hungry—but they had no place to go. They spent their first two nights sleeping on the ground outside a church in its garden area, surrounded by numerous other families trying to survive.

Realizing that Iraq held no future for his family, Zaki applied for visas to enter Jordan, and they soon became refugees in this neighboring country. His family found sanctuary within the narrow hallways of a church. For seven months they lived on the cement floor, with just a sheet to separate the living spaces between each family group that squeezed into this small space.

Until one day when his life was changed again.

The Foundation for Relief and Reconciliation in the Middle East (FRRME) is an organization that has a long history of providing aid to the people of the Middle East. Early in the crisis, FRRME sent staff members into Jordan to bring relief to the Iraqi refugees. Equipped with the love of Jesus and financial resources from caring supporters, they sought out people in need of help—and learned of the refugee families living in this desperate situation.

The staff offered the refugee families a spacious new place to call home, enabling them to live in community with the new friends they had come to love. Food, shelter and medical care would all be provided, if only the families were willing to trust them and to move.

Zaki was one of the first to say yes.

"God sent them to find me," Zaki explained. "I saw how these people helped us in the name of Jesus, and I realized I had been living wrong. I cleaned my heart for Jesus. Now I am always praying and reading my Bible."

The lesson from the Good Shepherd goes deep into Zaki's heart. He is teaching his children that Jesus loves them and will not forget them—the greatest love of all:

> "For this is what the Sovereign LORD says: 'I myself will search and find my sheep. I will be like a shepherd looking for his scattered flock. I will find my sheep and rescue them from all the places where they were scattered on that dark and cloudy day.'"
>
> Ezekiel 34:11–12 NLT

PAUSE TO PRAY

Thank You, Lord, that You are the Good Shepherd. I praise You that nothing and no one escapes Your notice. You care for every need. You go after the lost to rescue them and carry them home on Your shoulders.

Yahweh Ro'i, *I declare that all of Your promises prove true. Release Your words of life over those who desperately need Your help. I place my trust in You.*

Rescue the innocent from the hands of ISIS. You are a refuge to them in these times of trouble. You protect those who trust in Your name. May each one in need call upon You now, "The Lord Is My Shepherd." Thank You for Your promise to be with them and deliver them. You are their place of safety.

Raise up people who carry Your heart to see chains broken and prisoners set free. Show them what to do. Women, girls and children are being held in captivity and crying out to be released and reunited with their families. Rescue them and lift them up out of the pit of despair. Strengthen Your Church to move in compassion that acts, breaking off all feelings of helplessness, apathy and fear. May my heart beat as one with Yours.

In the powerful name of Jesus, "The Lord Is My Shepherd," I pray this in agreement with Your will in faith. Amen!

Pray to Release Perseverance for the People of God

"The LORD Is My Banner"
YAHWEH NISSI

And Moses built an altar and called its name,
The-LORD-Is-My-Banner.

Exodus 17:15

Lift it up! Raise it high! A victory is won!

An iconic photograph taken during World War II depicts six military servicemen raising a large American flag atop Mt. Suribachi on Iwo Jima. Seen below by the men engaged in the ongoing battle, this banner of pending victory brought a fresh wave of strength and renewed hope to the American troops. That is a powerful symbol!

The practice of carrying a banner into battle is said to have originated in ancient Egypt more than five thousand years ago. These banners, which could be observed from quite a distance, marked rallying points for the troops to receive direction and commands from their leaders.

Moses understood the power of the banner. When Israel faced its first military attack in the wilderness, Moses stood on top of a hill with the staff of God in his hands. As he raised the staff high over the battlefield, it served as a banner for everyone to see. We will look in the next section at Moses' strategy and the perseverance it required. It was after this battle that he built an altar, calling its name *Yahweh Nissi*, "The LORD Is My Banner."

Jesus foretold how He would become the banner of victory for all people when He went to the cross. He said, "And when I am lifted up from the earth, I will draw everyone to myself" (John 12:32 NLT). Through Jesus, sin is pardoned, death is disarmed—and the ultimate victory is won.

Praying for Perseverance in Conflict

Moses had a problem. His people were under assault from a new enemy—one that chose to begin a war without provocation.

> While the people of Israel were still at Rephidim, the warriors of Amalek attacked them. Moses commanded Joshua, "Choose some men to go out and fight the army of Amalek for us. Tomorrow, I will stand at the top of the hill, holding the staff of God in my hand." . . . As long as Moses held up the

staff in his hand, the Israelites had the advantage. But whenever he dropped his hand, the Amalekites gained the advantage.

Exodus 17:8–9, 11 NLT

When the Israelites came out of Egypt exhausted and weary, the Amalekites attacked. They targeted the people who were most vulnerable, the weakest ones who lagged behind at the back of the ranks. They had no fear of God (see Deuteronomy 25:17–19).

Moses decided to repeat a strategy that had worked successfully in the past. When Pharaoh and his armies pursued the children of Israel as they left Egypt, God told Moses to lift up his staff—"the staff of God" (Exodus 4:20 NIV)—to divide the waters of the Red Sea. The people passed through on dry ground, but Pharaoh's army was swallowed up by the sea.

Facing a new enemy, Moses chose to lift his staff once again. Did he expect it to be so hard?

After Moses directed Joshua to form an army, he went to the top of a hill to stand as an intercessor with the staff of God in his hands. As long as Moses kept the staff lifted up during the battle, Israel prevailed over the enemy. But Moses could not keep the staff raised high in his own strength.

He needed help.

When Moses became fatigued, Aaron and Hur came alongside him to provide support and keep his arms raised. As the two men held Moses' hands steady, Joshua and his army persevered to defeat the enemy.

Even those with the strongest faith benefit from the help and encouragement of others as they gain victory over the enemy.

The apostle Paul appealed strongly to the Christians in Rome to join him in praying that he would be rescued from unbelievers in Judea (see Romans 15:30–31). He repeated the same plea to the believers in Thessalonica, asking them to pray for his deliverance from wicked and evil people (2 Thessalonians 3:1–2).

Engaging in spiritual battles is difficult and requires perseverance to press through. When you pray for your brothers and sisters in the Middle East, it is as though you are holding up their arms so that, together as one, you will persevere until the victory is complete.

PAUSE TO PRAY

Thank You, Lord, that You are my banner. You are my hope. I place all my trust in You. Yahweh Nissi, I praise You for lifting up the banner of Your presence over me.

I invite Your purposes to be released as I join with my brothers and sisters in the Middle East in prayer. Remove every barrier, every obstacle and every objection that stands in the way, preventing Your will from being done on earth as it is in heaven.

As You lift up the banner of Your power and presence over Your people, may they look up! Raise their eyes to see above their natural circumstances and into the heavenly realm, where You rule and reign. Give them the tenacity to persevere until Your victory is complete. I stand with them in purpose and unity as Your glory is revealed. May the banner of Your glory come, even now.

In the powerful name of Jesus, "The Lord Is My Banner," I pray this in agreement with Your will in faith. Amen!

Releasing Strength through Perseverance

Up to two million refugees and Internally Displaced Persons (IDPs) came flooding into Kurdistan in the aftermath of ISIS's reign of terror in Iraq and Syria by the summer of 2015. With an overwhelming influx of people in desperate need of help, Christian workers and those assisting humanitarian aid organizations in the region felt the gravity of the situation as they took considerable risks to meet the pressing needs.

"God has established us here for such a time as this," said Billy Ray, Middle East director for World Orphans. "There has to be a people on the ground raising a banner saying, 'There's refuge here.'"

And that is what they are doing, both now and for the years ahead. World Orphans is one organization committed to standing with the refugees and IDPs to let them know, "You have a home here. You have a home in the heart of God." As followers of Jesus Christ, they feel obligated to serve the people with their whole hearts and with their lives.

This commitment often comes at a very high price.

Overwhelmed by human suffering, workers get tired—often becoming "frustrated, discouraged, numb, afraid and just plain fed up," a humanitarian worker in the Middle East told me, a man I will call Nathan. Many are separated from their own families at great distances for long periods of time. Concern for their personal safety looms over them as well, as attacks on aid workers more than tripled in the last decade.[1] Working under such high levels of stress can lead to anxiety, insomnia, fatigue, irritability, anger and depression. Post-traumatic stress disorder (PTSD) can be experienced by those who suffer through extraordinarily traumatic events.[2]

Nathan heard the bombs going off as he lay on his bed, shaking with fear. Every door was locked in the ramshackle apartment where he stayed. Objections of well-meaning people came flooding back through his mind.

"Why are you here? No one goes outside the Green Zone without security. You're going to get tortured or killed."

For the first time since becoming a dad, Nathan had ventured alone outside the safer region of Kurdistan into the volatile city of Baghdad. The sounds of war were just outside his door.

"I was really, really afraid," he said.

Nathan realized that if he was hurt or killed, it could ruin his son's life. Emotionally exhausted and overwhelmed, he reached his lowest point. In that moment, he forgot that his ultimate purpose in ministry was to see God's Kingdom break through. His strength needed to be renewed.

Back in California, a group of believers from an adult Sunday school class was praying for Nathan and his family. They had committed to support him in the work he was doing, and prayer was a primary piece of that support.

Profound, informed and insightful prayers were spoken in faith as the group met together. Prayers that demonstrated a deep understanding of what it means to follow Christ—being gracious, sacrificial, enemy-loving, placing the Kingdom of God above all else. Prayers spoken aloud and prayers written out for him to read.

He no longer felt alone.

The apostle Paul also experienced the hardships of ministry. In a letter written to the Corinthian church, Paul told them of the tremendous suffering he and his companions endured, "for we were so utterly burdened beyond our strength that we despaired of life itself" (2 Corinthians 1:8 ESV). In their distress, they trusted in God, who raises the dead—proof of His almighty power, infusing hope that He would act on their behalf again.

But that was not enough. Paul wanted something more. He wanted the help of the Church in prayer. "You also must help us by prayer, so that many will give thanks on our behalf for the blessing granted us through the prayers of many" (2 Corinthians 1:11 ESV). *The prayers of many.* No worker should stand alone.

PAUSE TO PRAY

Thank You, Lord, for the workers You have called and sent to the Middle East. They carry Your love and compassion into one of the darkest places on earth. Increase Your love in their hearts until it overflows. Send more workers into the harvest, for "the harvest is great, but the workers are few." I praise You, Yahweh Nissi, *for Your banner of love that stretches over them now.*

Thank You for being a refuge and strength for Your people, a present help to those who are facing times of trouble. When Your workers face frustration, discouragement and fatigue, surround them with Your presence, turning their frustration to peace, encouraging them with hope and renewing their strength as they wait on You.

Cancel every assignment the enemy has placed against them, as You shield them from harm and fill them with Your power. May they find their rest in You—rest that brings Your strength, joy and peace.

In the powerful name of Jesus, "The LORD *Is My Banner," I pray this in agreement with Your will in faith. Amen!*

Perseverance as God's Chosen End-Time Strategy

"First the Saturday People, then the Sunday People" is more than just a familiar slogan repeated in graffiti and chants throughout countries of the Middle East; it is a reality that continues to unfold as ISIS moves toward its ultimate goal to rid this strategic region of Christians and the influence of Christianity. As author Lela Gilbert explains in her book, *Saturday People, Sunday People*, it is in these Arab and Muslim countries that the "hatred of Jews is linked to hatred of Christians."[3]

Hatred was the underlying force that expelled nearly one million Jews from their homes and land in North Africa and the Middle East from 1948 to 1970. This ethnic cleansing stretched across Iraq, Yemen, Syria, Lebanon, Egypt, Libya, Algeria, Morocco and Tunisia, with catastrophic results. In many of these countries today, fewer than a hundred Jewish people remain.

As history begins to repeat itself—this time with the Christian population—believers in the West must wake up to see not just the humanitarian crisis that is unfolding, but also the prophetic and spiritual significance that is occurring with the decline of these ancient Christian communities.

What is the prophetic and spiritual significance of this region? Isaiah 11:11–12 sets the stage:

> It shall come to pass in that day that the Lord shall set His hand again the second time to recover the remnant of His people who are left, from Assyria and Egypt, from Pathros and Cush, from Elam and Shinar, from Hamath and the islands of the sea. He will set up a banner for the nations, and will assemble the outcasts of Israel, and gather

together the dispersed of Judah from the four corners of the earth.

Isaiah 11:11–12

In that history-setting day, the Lord will reach out His hand to "recover the remnant of His people who are left" from Iraq and Egypt, Ethiopia, Iran, Syria and the islands of the sea. "He will set up a banner for the nations," assembling the exiles from Israel and gathering the scattered people of Judah from the ends of the earth.

Jesus is the banner who is set before the nations. He is the "root of Jesse" in whom the Gentiles will hope (Romans 15:12). Both Jews and Gentiles will look upon Him and be gathered to Him.

Isaiah 19 describes what this will look like as the Lord makes Himself known. Egyptians will turn to Him in worship, and He will listen to their prayers and heal them. Egypt and Assyria (modern-day Iraq) will be connected by a highway where the people will move freely between their lands to worship God. Israel will join them to be a blessing in the earth, whom "The LORD of Hosts" will bless, saying, "Blessed is Egypt My people, and Assyria the work of My hands, and Israel My inheritance" (Isaiah 19:25).

Given the history of this region throughout the centuries and its current state of affairs, this is a remarkable prophetic word!

It is impossible to gather a remnant of people from a nation that has driven out the people group in its entirety. In order for this prophecy to be fulfilled, there must be a segment of His people who remain. The enemy knows this very well.

This is why the hatred of Jews is linked to the hatred of Christians—and this is why prayers for the perseverance of the people of God are so important.

─────────── PAUSE TO PRAY ───────────

Thank You, Lord, that You are the banner that one day all people will see. You are high and lifted up, and I declare that You are coming again!

I praise You that Your Word is true, and not one single word of Yours will fail. Your purposes will be fulfilled. Strengthen the remnant that remains in the Middle East as they prepare the way for Your return. I agree with Your Word and speak blessing over Egypt Your people, Assyria the work of Your hands and Israel Your inheritance.

Reveal Yourself through powerful dreams, visions and encounters so that Your people will hold fast to You, no matter what comes. You give the crown of life to those who remain faithful to You, even when facing death. I praise You that not even death can separate Your people from Your love.

In the powerful name of Jesus, "The LORD Is My Banner," I pray this in agreement with Your will in faith. Amen!

───────────────────────────────────

This spiritual battle is clearly seen in the natural world as ISIS is on the move. Through their persecution of the Church, ISIS fighters are helping to usher back the return of the Messiah as they scatter God's people until just the remnant remain.

In spite of all the pain, suffering and darkness, there is hope. Scripture is filled with prophetic words of promise that declare what will happen when Jesus the Messiah comes again:

In that day the LORD of hosts will be for a crown of glory
and a diadem of beauty to the remnant of His people.

Isaiah 28:5

Behold, He is coming with clouds, and every eye will see
Him, even they who pierced Him. And all the tribes of the
earth will mourn because of Him. Even so, Amen.

Revelation 1:7

"Behold, the dwelling place of God is with man. He will dwell
with them, and they will be his people, and God himself will
be with them as their God. He will wipe away every tear from
their eyes, and death shall be no more, neither shall there
be mourning, nor crying, nor pain anymore, for the former
things have passed away."

Revelation 21:3–4 ESV

"He who overcomes shall inherit all things, and I will be his
God and he shall be My son."

Revelation 21:7

These are the words to hold on to. They are the words
of life that bring hope and perseverance to the saints—the
remnant Jesus is coming back to reclaim.

Pray to Release
the Provision of God

"The LORD Will Provide"

YAHWEH YIREH

And Abraham called the name of the place, The-LORD-Will-Provide; as it is said to this day, "In the Mount of the LORD it shall be provided."

Genesis 22:14

"The Lord will provide." How many times have these words brought deep encouragement to the one in need? How beautiful that these simple words reflect the profound nature and character of God.

Abraham waited many years to inherit the promised provision of God for an heir. When he was one hundred years of age, his son Isaac was born—the son of the promise, the son he loved. When Isaac was still young, God tested Abraham and told him to take this son to the mountains of Moriah to sacrifice him as a burnt offering.

Abraham obeyed God without question. In faith he believed that God would bring Isaac back to life (see Hebrews 11:19). Just as Abraham was lifting up the knife in his hand to slay his son on the altar, a voice from heaven stopped him. Abraham found a ram to sacrifice as an offering instead of his son and called that place *Yahweh Yireh*, "The LORD Will Provide."

In Hebrew the word *yireh* is translated as "provide." It is based on the root word *ra'ah*, which means "to see." It embraces the concept of having vision to perceive, to consider, to regard. In English, the word *provide* is formed from two Latin root words that together mean "to see ahead."

God, who knows all things from beginning to end, sees ahead before a problem even arises and makes provision for its needs.

Before the foundation of the world, God saw ahead to the need of mankind for a Savior. The directive to sacrifice Isaac, the only son of promise, foreshadowed the ultimate sacrifice that would be made of Jesus, the only Son of God.

Yahweh Yireh, "The Lord Will Provide." On the cross, Jesus, God in the flesh, was seen by all who passed by. The Father provided a perfect and sinless sacrifice to take away the sins of the world and reconcile mankind back to Himself.

Through Jesus, provision is complete.

Releasing Provision for Physical Needs

Within the first year of ISIS's rise to power in 2014, more than 3.3 million people were displaced from their homes in Iraq, with 7.6 million Internally Displaced Persons fleeing inside Syria as a result of the ongoing civil war and ISIS's presence. These numbers do not reflect the countless others that escaped to neighboring countries, creating one of the largest refugee exoduses in recent history. By 2015 one third of the world's refugees came from Iraq and Syria alone. And the crisis continues to grow.[1]

The needs are great.

During the displacement, many people were unable to find shelter in the limited IDP camps, which led them to occupy any space they could find in schools, churches, unfinished or abandoned buildings. Those who found temporary homes in the camps faced extreme hardship as well, with limited access to food, clean water, basic necessities and sanitary living conditions.

In 2015 more than 630,000 people were housed in these emergency shelter arrangements throughout Iraq. Ten percent of the entire 3.3 million displaced population group continued to live in unfinished and abandoned buildings.

"Misery has become a permanent resident in these camps," said Dr. Sarah Ahmed, a humanitarian worker with FRRME. "With the passage of time, I see more sadness and more changes. Defining home as a camp is taking a toll."

Soaring temperatures in the summer render the very young, the old and the weak at extreme risk for heat stroke, dehydration and death. Prolonged exposure to frigid temperatures and snow in the winter creates the risk of hypothermia.

When facing a catastrophe that creates such immense need, the temptation is to turn away from the problem, because it looms with impossibility. Praise God that what is impossible for man is possible with Him. He chooses to equip the Church to "do good by meeting the urgent needs of others" (Titus 3:14 NLT), creating an avenue to put faith into action. This is where faith gets to shine!

"A Christ-follower's first response in a crisis is to always take seriously the responsibility to listen—and not turn away," Ann Voskamp wrote on her blog, *A Holy Experience*.[2]

She pushed aside the fears of those who pleaded with her to stay home, to stay where she was safe—the fear that was her own. "Sometimes we all just have to unlearn fear to learn to love."

Ann boarded a plane for Erbil, Iraq, and went to the refugee camp, where she stood among the beautiful families that had fled from ISIS and instability and war.

She looked into the eyes of the traumatized father and listened as he told the story of his family. When an ISIS bomb exploded beside their house, he grabbed his family as they ran for their lives, leaving everything behind.

In a whisper he confided their hopes and dreams, "We just want to go home."

She sat with a group of Yazidi mothers in a shipping container. This was where they slept with their children—this was now their temporary home. She listened of the horrors each mother had faced. They ran from ISIS in the middle of the night, taking their children up Mount Sinjar as they tried to escape.

"ISIS shot her husband. Then they shot her son," the woman said of her sister, who sat next to Ann.

ISIS took everything they had, destroying their homes then destroying their lives.

Ann determined that these women would not carry this terror alone. "How does the church not stand up and howl?"

She came home with a goal to raise $150,000 for the Preemptive Love Coalition—a goal that would put Iraqi children back into school, a goal that would empower women with start-up business grants. A goal to bring hope back once again.

Ann did not stand up alone. The Church stood with her.

Within hours her goal was met, and the contributions kept coming in. Three days later, half a million dollars had been raised. And it did not stop there, as believers continued to release provision for their brothers and sisters in the Middle East.

Faith moved into action as sacrificial love poured out to meet the urgent need.

The church in Philippi understood sacrificial giving. At the beginning of Paul's ministry, no other church took care of meeting his needs—but the Philippians sent him help more than once. They shared in his trouble. They continued to give while his need existed.

As a result their gifts were received as "a fragrant offering, a sacrifice acceptable and pleasing to God" (Philippians 4:18 ESV).

And as a result God would supply all their needs by His glorious riches in Christ Jesus.

——————————— PAUSE TO PRAY ———————————

Thank You, Lord, that You are Yahweh Yireh, *the God of infinite provision. I declare that in You, there is more than enough to meet every need!*

I praise You that You have seen ahead to these times of trouble and give Your full attention to release provision to those who are suffering. You said that the fast You have chosen is that I share my food with the hungry, provide shelter for the poor, give clothes to the naked and not turn away from those in need.[3]

You release provision through my hands, as You give me ability to meet the needs You set before me. Help me not to turn away. May my eyes always be focused on You and never on my own perception of lack. Keep me from holding on to selfishness in my heart. Thank You that when I respond to the needs of the least of these, my gifts are received as an offering to You.

Move in the hearts of Your people to respond in this time of crisis. Mobilize the efforts of churches, Christian organizations and the international community to join in the relief work and not hold back anything within their ability to help. May we all work in unison with You to release Your provision and care, standing in the face of injustice to do what is right.

In the powerful name of Jesus, "The LORD Will Provide," I pray this in agreement with Your will in faith. Amen!

Releasing Provision for Emotional Needs

It was our first encounter with Iraqi hospitality. My husband, Gabriel, and I had traveled to Jordan to meet with the Christian refugees who had fled from ISIS—to listen to their stories, to learn from them, to pray with them.

We were brought to the balcony of an apartment building that stood next door to a mosque. Heavy blankets were hung from the rafters to block out the noise and provide a semblance of privacy.

The balcony was quickly filled to capacity with Iraqis who had come to worship the Lord together. It was the highlight of their week.

When the worship service was over, we were invited into the apartment to enjoy an authentic Iraqi meal. The table was teeming with a variety of foods and many dishes I had never seen before. Platter after platter continued to be placed in front of us. It was obvious that great care and preparation had been made for our time together.

When we had finished eating, we learned a surprising detail about the man who had prepared this feast. Years ago he was the personal chef for Saddam Hussein.

"Did Saddam hire the chef because he knew that as a Christian, the chef could be trusted not to poison him?" I teased.

I was completely surprised when the answer came back, "Yes!"

To the Iraqis gathered in the room, this fact was common knowledge.

Saddam's fear of being poisoned ran so deep that he brought his personal chef with him on his travels to Egypt, Yemen, Saudi Arabia and Kuwait. There was a valid reason for his fear. In 1996 one of the chef's colleagues was caught trying to poison the dictator. The man was executed immediately.

Now the chef lives in Jordan as a refugee.

We met many other professionals that day. University professors, business owners, scientists and teachers—these were the fortunate ones who found safety in Jordan after they fled from ISIS. It is here they wait month after month to receive news of visa approvals from host countries in the West, so they may start their lives again.

While the refugees wait, they are forbidden to work without legal permits, which are extremely difficult—and in some cases impossible—to obtain. If they are caught working illegally, they are subject to stiff fines and deportation. Depleted of all resources, the refugees are wholly dependent on others for food, shelter and the basic necessities of living.

Without an opportunity to utilize their skills and training, many refugees succumb to the boredom and mental anguish that waiting can bring. This suffering is often compounded by the trauma they have faced as they seek to heal from emotional wounds.

When purpose is lost, hopelessness is not far behind.

Nasim was starting to go blind. Like so many others, he desperately wanted to find purpose in his new life in Jordan. After receiving prayer from his pastor and leaders, his vision began to improve—and out of the darkness, hope began to emerge.

He always knew that Jesus meant everything to him, but now he experienced His presence in a life-changing way. Nasim began to accompany his pastor on visits to the other refugee families. He wanted others to know what Jesus had done for him, encouraging them with the Word of God.

In suffering, his purpose was found.

"My suffering was good for me, for it taught me to pay attention to your decrees" (Psalm 119:71 NLT).

"God is raising up leaders," said Richard Sherrod, a Christian minister who provides relief and spiritual comfort to the refugees in Jordan. "The transformation from victim to victor mentality is a journey.

"The key to transformation," Richard explained, "is when people see the goodness of God."

In Psalm 23:5 David uses poetic imagery to portray the goodness of God through His provision that touches the needs of body and soul. "You prepare a table before me in the presence of my enemies; you anoint my head with oil; my cup overflows" (ESV). David was not just given a meal but presented with a feast. The table was not laid out in the presence of his friends when life was peaceful but in the presence of his enemies when life was in turmoil.

And yet he was given all he needed.

His head was anointed with oil—oil that was poured out to anoint kings and priests, oil that was used to anoint the sick. No wonder his cup overflowed with blessings!

PAUSE TO PRAY

Thank You, Lord, for Your unfailing love. You see each one in need and You care about the anguish of each soul. Yahweh Yireh, in these times of suffering, release Your blessing until it overflows.

For the refugees who have left their countries behind, may they find their hope in You. Remind Your people that their citizenship is in heaven, where every spiritual blessing is theirs. Give them focused vision to look to You for the release of purpose and destiny as their lives begin again. Raise up leaders among them who will encourage others with Your words of life. May they see Your goodness and experience Your kindness as You refresh their souls.

Bring comfort to those who are dealing with loss and the upheaval of change. Keep them from the torment of reliving painful memories. Heal the wounds caused by emotional trauma as You anoint their heads with oil. May all who are suffering find their rest in You.

In the powerful name of Jesus, "The LORD *Will Provide," I pray this in agreement with Your will in faith. Amen!*

Releasing Provision for Spiritual Needs

Unexpectedly, armed terrorists came into the laboratory in Baghdad where Ammar was working as a chemical engineer. At first, they came looking for his manager. When they discovered Ammar was a Christian, they took him away, too.

"At that time, I felt I was very close to my death," he said.

Ammar was afraid. Yet in his fear, he was reassured in the knowledge that he was a child of God. Ammar trusted in Him.

One day as he was being moved to a new location, a battle broke out between ISIS and resistance forces. Ammar was set free. In that moment Ammar experienced the powerful hand of God.

"When He said, 'I will not leave or forsake you,'" Ammar explained, "He proved that to me on a personal level."

God's promises are everlasting.

Ammar prays for the ones who took him captive. He knows they are far from the God of truth. It is only through an encounter with the true God that change will take place.

"A person who has not encountered Christ or experienced Him cannot know the love, mercy and many blessings of God," he said. "I pray that God, who changed the soul of Paul the apostle, will change the souls of all these people who persecute Christ and His Church."

It was Paul who spoke to the men of Athens regarding the spiritual need God has placed in every heart. God puts people in specific times and places "that they should seek God," in the hope that they might "feel their way toward him and find him." Each person was created with the spiritual need to know God and be known by Him, though He is "actually not far from each one of us" (Acts 17:27 ESV).

Jesus addressed the deep spiritual needs that only He can meet through an encounter with a Samaritan woman at Jacob's well.

She came near to draw water. He came to give her life. "Everyone who drinks this water will be thirsty again," He told her, "but whoever drinks the water I give them will never thirst. Indeed, the water I give them will become in them a spring of water welling up to eternal life" (John 4:13–14 NIV).

Intrigued by the thought of living water, she asked for a drink. She never wanted to be thirsty again.

Jesus told her to go call her husband and come back. She responded she was not married, a truth He already knew. Jesus said she had been married five times before, and that she was living with a man though not married to him.

This prophetic word of knowledge was the key that unlocked her heart.

In Jesus she found the Messiah she was waiting for—and she gained the love, acceptance, forgiveness and purpose that filled her deepest spiritual needs.

Through her encounter with Jesus, lasting change took place.

She ran back to her village to tell everyone about Jesus—the Man who told her everything she ever did. Her words were convincing. People came streaming out of the village to go meet Jesus for themselves.

As the people drew near, Jesus said to His disciples, "I tell you, open your eyes and look at the fields! They are ripe for harvest" (John 4:35 NIV).

The transformation of one led to a harvest of souls.

 PAUSE TO PRAY

Thank You, Lord, that You provide for the needs of the body, soul and spirit. I praise You, Yahweh Yireh, that You supply every spiritual blessing in Christ. Release Your spiritual blessings now.

Come and pour out Your Spirit on Your people who have been persecuted for Your name's sake. Draw near to hear their whispered prayers as You release provision to meet their deepest spiritual needs. Fill them to overflowing with Your love and joy.

Thank You, Lord, that You have created all people with an instinctive need for You. You are not far off but within reach. Bring those who persecute the Church to their knees in a powerful encounter with Your presence. May You transform their hearts as they transform their lives.

In the powerful name of Jesus, "The LORD Will Provide," I pray this in agreement with Your will in faith. Amen!

Pray to Release
the Healing of God

> **"The LORD Who Heals"**
> *YAHWEH RAPHA*

"For I am the LORD who heals you."

Exodus 15:26

How great is God's love for humanity! He revealed His first redemptive and covenantal name to the Israelites coming out of captivity as *Yahweh Rapha*, "The LORD Who Heals." Before God was revealed as their Shepherd—before they knew Him as their Provider or as the One who would bring them peace—He made His compassion known through His promise to be their Healer.

For hundreds of years, the entire nation had suffered the cruelty of slavery in Egypt. Their present trauma was not the result of stories passed down from former generations; it was the personal experience of every man, woman and child coming out of Egypt. This nation that now knew freedom was in great need of healing to bind up its wounds.

The Israelites did not know that God was about to reveal Himself in a powerful way again. They had made their escape from Egypt through the parting of the Red Sea. But now they were thirsty after three days of walking in the wilderness without water—and when they finally did find a source of water, it was bitter and unsuitable for drinking.

Moses took their complaint to the Lord, and God gave him the solution. At His direction, Moses took a tree and threw it into the water. The water became sweet.

As God healed the water, He would heal His people. "I will put none of the diseases on you which I have brought on the Egyptians. For I am the LORD who heals you" (Exodus 15:26).

Through His name *Yahweh Rapha*, God reveals the provision He has made for healing—provision that Jesus made complete through His atoning death on the cross.

The suffering of the coming Messiah was prophesied in Isaiah 53:5: "But He was wounded for our transgressions, He was bruised for our iniquities; the chastisement for our peace was upon Him, and by His stripes we are healed." Healing is spoken of in the present tense. On the cross, Jesus, the Messiah, paid the penalty for our sin and made provision for our physical healing as He "took our illnesses and bore our diseases" (Matthew 8:17 ESV).

In compassionate love and mercy, God the Father sent His only beloved Son to redeem the world back to Himself.

Through Jesus' obedient sacrifice, He provides freedom from the curse of sin, sickness and death.

The Father is not simply compassionate—He is full of compassion. His compassion knows no limits.

How deep the Father's love!

Releasing the Promise for Physical Healing

The young widow was in pain. She tried to cope with the debilitating side effects of an internal illness that had damaged her liver and gallbladder, but the pain had become too intense. Doctors and medicines had not been able to help. Her pain was compounded by the loneliness it created, isolating her from the other refugee families who were living in Jordan.

In her kitchen she cried out to the Lord.

Suddenly she no longer felt alone. The presence of the Lord had descended into the room.

"If this is really You, God, please show me," she wept. "I want You. You're all I have. I have nothing else."

She felt the warmth of a touch on her back. She knew it was a touch from God.

Immediately her pain was significantly lessened. She felt His peace, which became her own. It was something she could not keep to herself. She had to tell everyone she knew!

One encounter with the living God changed her entire viewpoint. One encounter that reminded her of the power of His presence—one encounter that reminded her of the promise of His love.

Studies have shown that people who have experienced trauma are often at a higher risk to develop chronic physical pain, brought on by the stress and emotional issues they face. This in turn can lead to feelings of hopelessness, anxiety and depression.[1]

Those who have medical needs in the IDP and refugee camps located throughout Iraq, Syria, Jordan and Turkey face many challenges. Overcrowding in the camps and a shortage of workers compromise access to even basic health care. Hospital service in many areas is limited and often interrupted, as periodic closures occur due to the ongoing threat of ISIS attacks.

Even those who arrive in a good state of health are at risk in the camps. Food shortages lead to malnutrition and anemia; lack of safe drinking water and inadequate sanitation facilities contribute to outbreaks of disease.

The need for physical healing is overwhelming.

Jesus did not let His own personal encounter with loss prevent Him from responding compassionately to people in need. When He heard that his cousin John the Baptist had been beheaded, He withdrew in a boat to a remote area to be alone. But the crowds heard where He was headed, and they came out from many towns to follow Him (see Matthew 14:1–14).

Compassion for the sick moved Jesus into action.

Seeing the large crowds, He stepped out of His boat onto the shore. He came to heal the sick. Praise God that "Jesus Christ is the same yesterday, today, and forever" (Hebrews 13:8). The compassion that moved Him to heal people then is the compassion that moves Him to heal people still.

Jesus started a healing revolution. The dictionary defines the word *revolution* as "a fundamental change in the way of thinking about something; a change in paradigm." His ability and willingness to heal drew crowds wherever He went. It even drew the attention of His adversaries; they questioned Jesus about the source of His authority as He released healing to the people (see Matthew 21:23–27). *All* were astonished at the majesty of God (see Luke 9:37–43).

Jesus then commissioned His disciples to go and do the same. He gave them authority and power to cast out demons and heal every kind of disease and illness. He commanded them to "heal the sick, cleanse the lepers, raise the dead, cast out demons. Freely you have received, freely give" (Matthew 10:8). His healing revolution grew.

At His final Passover supper on the night He was betrayed, Jesus made a promise for His healing revolution to continue after He was gone. He said to His disciples, "I tell you the truth, anyone who believes in me will do the same works I have done, and even greater works, because I am going to be with the Father" (John 14:12 NLT). Anyone who believes in Jesus will do not just the same works that He did but even greater works. *Anyone!*

PAUSE TO PRAY

Thank You, Lord, that You are full of compassion. I praise You, Yahweh Rapha, *that it is Your compassionate love that moves Your heart and releases Your healing to people in need.*

Fill my heart with Your compassion as Your desires become my own. Teach me how to see as You see and to love as You love. Let faith rise up in me to believe the promise Jesus made that I will do the works that He did because I believe in Him—and then let my faith be put into action.

Stretch out Your hand to heal those in the Middle East who are suffering from sickness, disease and physical pain. You call each one by name—each one is continuously in

Your thoughts. Send help and healing to those who have no other hope but You. Strengthen the immune system of every person living in the refugee camps. Remind them all of Your unfailing love as You meet their every need.

In the powerful name of Jesus, "The LORD Who Heals," I pray this in agreement with Your will in faith. Amen!

Healing the Pain of Emotional Trauma

In the early morning hours of August 3, 2014, ISIS militants invaded the Iraqi villages surrounding Mount Sinjar, forcing more than three hundred thousand Yazidi men, women and children to flee from their homes.[2] The violence was horrific. Hundreds of men were slaughtered on the streets. Scores of women and girls were abducted and given as wives to ISIS fighters or sold into sexual slavery in open markets.

To escape from the mass killings and kidnapping spree, more than forty thousand Yazidis made their way up to the top of Mount Sinjar. Surrounded by ISIS fighters in the villages below, the people were stranded without food, water and medical care in the heat of a scorching desert. Many children died of dehydration, leaving their families to bury them in shallow graves, covering their bodies with stones.[3]

"The offensive on the mountain was as much a sexual conquest as it was for territorial gain," said Matthew Barber, a University of Chicago expert on the Yazidi minority.[4] The campaign to kidnap and enslave Yazidi females was a deliberate and pre-planned event.

Through this event, ISIS formally introduced sexual slavery as it elevated its theology of rape. Although Yazidi women were specifically targeted for sexual slavery, the rape of Christian and Jewish women captured in battle was also given sanction by ISIS leadership.[5] Bolstered by internal policy memos, theological discussions and an extensive how-to manual issued by Islamic State Research and the Fatwa Department, ISIS leadership emphasized a narrow and selective reading of the Quran to justify this brutal practice. Sexual conquests were seen as victories to celebrate; rape became a beneficial act that served to draw the men closer to their god.

"Every time that he came to rape me, he would pray," said one fifteen-year-old girl who was kidnapped from Mount Sinjar and sold to a fighter.[6] Systematic rape was considered his act of worship.

The enslavement of women and girls became a staple for ISIS leadership to reward jihadists and to attract new recruits.

"Traumatized people feel utterly abandoned, utterly alone, cast out of the human and divine systems of care and protection that sustain life," writes Dr. Judith Herman in her book, *Trauma and Recovery*.[7] "Traumatic events shatter the sense of connection between individual and community, creating a crisis of faith."

Questions about God and His role in the traumatic event are inevitable. "How could a loving God allow such a horrific tragedy?" and "Where is God in times of human pain and suffering?" are questions often asked by trauma survivors, along with the watching world.

In addition to feelings of abandonment and experiencing a crisis of faith, traumatic events cause generalized anxiety and specific fears. Traumatized individuals sometimes relive the event as though it is occurring again in the present or experience it again through nightmares. They often feel a sense of alienation from others, as all of their relationships are affected and usually damaged. Feelings of survivor guilt can be overwhelming.

Traumatic events that cause emotional pain also cause physical pain that can continue to be experienced in the body.

"The body holds trauma," says Michelle Matson, a counselor who specializes in cases of trauma and abuse. "Trauma takes time to work itself out, both in the mind and in the body."

David was well acquainted with emotional distress. As a young shepherd, he struck down lions and bears as he protected his flocks. He battled giants and was often surrounded by enemies in battle that sought to take his life. He was pursued relentlessly by the king, so he hid in forests and in caves. He feigned madness to save his life. Even his beloved son Absalom plotted his death.[8]

In these times of despair, David cried out to the Lord. The Psalms are filled with his desperate prayers to be seen, to be heard, to be rescued from his misery.

> My eyes are always on the LORD, for he rescues me from the traps of my enemies. Turn to me and have mercy, for I am alone and in deep distress. My problems go from bad to worse. Oh, save me from them all! Feel my pain and see my trouble. Forgive all my sins. See how many enemies I have and how viciously they hate me! Protect me! Rescue my life from them! Do not let me be disgraced, for in you I take refuge.
>
> Psalm 25:15–20 NLT

In times of greatest emotional pain, his eyes were on the Lord.

In times of greatest emotional pain, the eyes of the Lord were upon him.

"Every human being has the desire and the need to be seen," said counselor Michelle Matson, conveying a truth she has witnessed through her work with trauma and abuse victims. "Am I seen? Am I known?"

That is the power of the gaze—the power that affirms, "You are not alone."

Thank You, Lord, that You see each person who is experiencing emotional pain and that You are intimately aware of every need. You are not a God who is distant and aloof, but You are near to all who call on Your name. I praise You, Yahweh Rapha, for Your extravagant love that heals the wounds of every shattered heart. Release Your healing now.

So many people have been traumatized by the atrocities of ISIS. When their hearts are overwhelmed, reconnect them to You. Bring those who feel abandoned out of the pit of despair. May they feel Your eyes upon them as they lift their eyes to You. Calm each anxious thought and remove each paralyzing fear. Thank You for being their refuge and strength, their very present help in times of trouble.

Breathe fresh courage into their hearts as You strengthen their souls with joy. May they find healing through relationships with others and healing through their relationship with You. Renew their hope as You restore them to health. I praise You that all who search for You will be filled with joy!

In the powerful name of Jesus, "The LORD Who Heals," I pray this in agreement with Your will in faith. Amen!

Releasing God's Healing to the Nations

So often when healing comes to mind, it is centered on restoring wholeness to an individual. But God's heart reaches beyond the individual to the nations as well. "On each side of the river stood the tree of life, bearing twelve crops of fruit, yielding its fruit every month. And the leaves of the tree are for the healing of the nations" (Revelation 22:2 NIV). Even at the end of time, God's heart is turned toward the nations as He makes provision for their healing.

A striking parallel can be seen in the first Psalm.

> Oh, the joys of those who do not follow the advice of the wicked, or stand around with sinners, or join in with mockers. But they delight in the law of the LORD, meditating on it day and night. They are like trees planted along the riverbank, bearing fruit each season. Their leaves never wither, and they prosper in all they do.
>
> Psalm 1:1–3 NLT

In this passage the psalmist says that the people who delight in God's instructions, who meditate on His Word day and night, are like trees planted on the riverbank bearing fruit in season—*with leaves that never wither*. Does this sound familiar? Could it be that the provision God has made for the healing of the nations is to come through His people who take joy in following His advice? Will He release healing through your prayers—healing through your actions?

"And they prosper in all they do."

God has given the responsibility to the Church to pray and intercede for all people, including national leaders and authorities (see 1 Timothy 2:1–4). This is His instruction. His purpose is twofold. First, prayers for those who are in authority release our ability to "live peaceful and quiet lives in all godliness and holiness" (1 Timothy 2:2 NIV). Second, this type of prayer is pleasing to God as the Church stands in agreement with His will for "all people to be saved and to come to a knowledge of the truth" (1 Timothy 2:4 NIV).

Prayers must be made by those who are in right relationship with God and in right relationship with others. Psalm 66:18 says, "If I regard iniquity in my heart, the LORD will not hear." Relationship with God begins with humility of heart.

A right relationship with others is broken if there is unwillingness to forgive. This attitude can hinder prayers. Jesus said, "Whenever you stand praying, forgive, if you have anything against anyone" (Mark 11:25 ESV).

In a German concentration camp, surrounded by suffering and cruelty, Corrie ten Boom began to learn the power of forgiveness that releases healing. In her book *The Hiding Place* (Chosen, 2006), Corrie described how her most joy-filled days in captivity were those with her sister, Betsie, when they would sit in their flea-infested barracks and intercede for all the people in the camp, guards and prisoners alike. But their prayers did not stop there.

"We prayed beyond the concrete walls for the healing of Germany, of Europe, of the world," wrote Corrie. The sisters understood their responsibility to stand in the gap through prayer for the healing of the nations.

After the war, Corrie found herself face-to-face with one of her former S.S. prison guards—a man who did not remember her; a man she could not forget. He reached out to shake her hand. He was amazed at her message of God's love and forgiveness, and grateful to realize his sins were washed away. Corrie's hand stayed by her side.

On her own she did not have the strength to forgive. Corrie asked Jesus to give her His forgiveness for this man. She took her former captor's hand, and Jesus supplied the miracle. His overwhelming love filled her heart.

"And so I discovered that it is not on our forgiveness any more than on our goodness that the world's healing hinges, but on His," said Corrie.

--- **PAUSE TO PRAY** ---

Thank You, Lord, that Your heart is turned to the healing of the nations. You have given each nation an inheritance and a purpose to fulfill—a purpose to seek after You and to find You. I praise You, Yahweh Rapha, for the provision of healing that is released through Your name. You heal people and You heal nations.

As You bind up the wounds of the people, may You bind up the wounds of the nations in the Middle East. May these nations learn to know You as the one true God, for You desire all people to be saved and come to the knowledge of the truth.

Thank You that as they fear Your name, healing is released—healing through forgiveness, healing through Your Son. You desire for the nations to be glad and sing for joy, because You govern the nations with justice as You guide them on the earth. May Your healing flow.

In the powerful name of Jesus, "The Lord Who Heals," I pray this in agreement with Your will in faith. Amen!

Pray to Release
the Peace of God

So Gideon built an altar there to the LORD, and called
it The-LORD-Is-Peace.

Judges 6:24

Peace. For those who lived in the United States during the
1960s and '70s, the word *peace* probably calls to mind the
"peace sign" hand gesture, or inspires visions of long-haired
hippies in tie-dyed T-shirts with the peace symbol splashed
across their chests.

For many this word was synonymous with the absence of war. It was a time when limits were few and self-expression thrived. Symbols of peace were everywhere—but true peace was noticeably absent from many hearts.

In Hebrew the word for "peace" is *shalom*. It encompasses so much more than a state of tranquility or absence of war. *Shalom* embraces welfare for the body in safety, health and prosperity, and welfare for the soul in contentment, tranquility and rest. *Shalom* is derived from the verb *shalam*, which means "to restore what is missing to bring wholeness and completeness." In *shalom*, there is nothing missing or lacking—and nothing added that does not belong.

The first introduction of God's name *Yahweh Shalom* appears in the book of Judges when Gideon was visited by the angel of the Lord. Things were not going well for Gideon. The people of Israel had done evil in the sight of God, and as a result, God had given them over to their enemies for seven years.

The angel brought a blessing—a confirmation that the Lord was with him—but Gideon was confused. "If the LORD is with us, why then has all this happened to us?" (Judges 6:13). It is a question that has been asked through the ages.

The angel of the Lord commissioned Gideon to be the one who would save Israel from their enemies. Gideon was not so sure. He needed a sign.

Gideon prepared an offering of meat and unleavened cakes and brought it to the angel of the Lord. In front of Gideon's eyes, the angel tipped his staff to touch the rocks on which the offering lay. Fire sprang up and consumed the meat and cakes. The angel of the Lord vanished from his sight.

It was then Gideon realized he had been visited by an angel and not by a man. Fear gripped his heart. But the Lord said to him, "Peace be with you; do not fear, you shall not die"

(Judges 6:23). So Gideon built an altar to the Lord there, and called it "The LORD Is Peace."

Yahweh Shalom became his peace, restoring what was missing from his heart.

When an angel announced the Messiah's birth to the shepherds in the fields, he was suddenly accompanied by "a multitude of the heavenly host praising God and saying, 'Glory to God in the highest, and on earth peace among those with whom he is pleased!'" (Luke 2:13–14 ESV).

Jesus the Messiah came to earth as the Prince of Peace—to restore what was missing and lacking, bringing wholeness and completeness back to humankind.

Finding Peace in Times of Suffering

Scripture gives many promises that are comforting and encouraging. Here is one promise that on the surface does not seem to be one of them: "Yes, and all who desire to live godly in Christ Jesus will suffer persecution" (2 Timothy 3:12). After all, who looks forward to persecution? Is this not something everyone wants to avoid?

The interviewer asked his question in all sincerity. "How can Christians in America pray for believers in China?" He did not anticipate the leader's response.

"Stop praying for persecution in China to end," the leader responded, "for it is through persecution that the Church has grown."[1]

In the presence of persecution, believers hold on to the One who gives them peace.

Jesus did not promise that those who follow Him will have a life of ease. On His final night with His disciples, He told them that they would face persecution, for a servant is not greater than his master. If Jesus Himself was persecuted, they could expect the same. To keep them from falling away, Jesus promised to send the Helper—the Holy Spirit—who would guide them into all truth and tell them of things to come.

Jesus told His disciples, "I have said these things to you, that in me you may have peace. In the world you will have tribulation. But take heart; I have overcome the world" (John 16:33 ESV).

The One who spoke peace to calm the wind and the waves stood before them as "The LORD Is Peace," the One who calms hearts.

Church history documents that all but one of Jesus' disciples were martyred for their faith. James was the first to be executed by the sword. When Herod saw it pleased the religious leaders, he proceeded to arrest Peter with the same intent in mind. "Peter was therefore kept in prison, but constant prayer was offered to God for him by the church" (Acts 12:5).

The church gathered together to pray for Peter through the night. Through their prayers, God released angelic help to guide him safely out of prison.

While the prayer meeting was taking place, Peter was sleeping between two soldiers and bound by chains. An angel appeared in his cell and struck Peter on his side, waking him. The chains fell off his hands.

The angel told Peter to get dressed quickly and follow him. Peter thought he was experiencing a vision. He did not realize that the angel was real.

It was only after they had passed two more guard posts and gone through the iron gates of the city—gates that opened automatically when they came near—that Peter realized the Lord had sent an angel to rescue him (see Acts 12:1–19).

The hand of the Lord had been on Peter to lead him out in peace. Wholeness and completeness. Nothing missing, nothing lacking—nothing added that did not belong. *Shalom.*

"Peace I leave with you, My peace I give to you; not as the world gives do I give to you. Let not your heart be troubled, neither let it be afraid" (John 14:27).

———— PAUSE TO PRAY ————

Thank You, Lord, that You bless Your people with peace. Yahweh Shalom, *I praise You that Your peace restores what is missing to bring wholeness and completeness to the body, soul and spirit.*

God of all comfort, extend Your peace to Your people who are suffering and facing persecution in the Middle East because they hold fast to the name of Jesus. May Your peace envelop them and give them strength, exceeding their understanding as Your peace guards their hearts and minds. Thank You that Your thoughts toward them are thoughts of peace, to give them a future and a hope. Impart Your peace deeply into their hearts.

Speak Your peace also into the evil hearts of ISIS fighters who persecute others with ruthless cruelty. Captivate their attention until all they see is You and the power of the cross. As they are confronted by Your love, may they reach out to receive the forgiveness You extend. Transform them by Your grace.

In the powerful name of Jesus, "The LORD Is Peace," I pray this in agreement with Your will in faith. Amen!

Pursuing Peace in the Middle East

As long as people have lived on the earth, there has been conflict in the Middle East. From the beginning, with Cain's murder of his brother Abel, to the current unrest between factions of Arabs and Jews, Christians and Muslims, Sunnis and Shi'as, the nations of the Middle East have a long and sordid history of strife, infighting, war and bloodshed.

Into this turmoil, the Prince of Peace arrived. For hundreds of years, the Jewish people had been waiting for their promised Messiah to appear. When Jesus came to them, their hearts were fixed on a leader who would overthrow the Roman government and forever free Israel from dominance and oppression. For this reason, when Jesus rode into Jerusalem seated on a donkey, the crowds shouted, "Hosanna! 'Blessed is He who comes in the name of the LORD!' Blessed is the kingdom of our father David!" (Mark 11:9–10). The people limited their expectations to God's military peace on earth; Jesus came to bring Kingdom peace that was eternal.

And so to His people struggling with conflict and unrest, the Prince of Peace taught the way of peace.

Jesus said, "Love your enemies, bless those who curse you, do good to those who hate you, and pray for those who spitefully use you and persecute you, that you may be sons of your Father in heaven" (Matthew 5:44–45). He became the living example of this word as He hung from the cross. "Father, forgive them, for they do not know what they do" (Luke 23:34).

When Jesus walked the earth, He sent out His disciples before Him into the cities and places He would go. He sent them to usher in the Kingdom of God—He sent them carrying

His peace. "But whatever house you enter, first say, 'Peace to this house'" (Luke 10:5). Jesus taught them that His peace, which they carried, could be multiplied to others as it was given away and received.

Jesus said, "Blessed are the peacemakers, for they shall be called sons of God" (Matthew 5:9). Not only were His disciples to carry His peace, but those who pursued His peace would become peacemakers.

"Fighting for peace in the Middle East is always hard," writes Canon Andrew White in his book *The Vicar of Baghdad* (Monarch, 2009), "but at times in Iraq it is soul-destroying."

A modern-day peacemaker, Canon White spent years in the Middle East gaining extensive experience in conflict mediation. Through his work, he learned that peacemaking can be summarized in one word: *love*.

"It is love that leads us to forgiveness," says Canon White. "Jesus taught us to love our enemies, but generally, we do not like them very much. So much of my time is spent with unpleasant people, and so before I approach them I simply pray: 'Lord, help me to love them!'"

That is a prayer He will not deny.

"If possible, so far as it depends on you, be at peace with all men" (Romans 12:18 NASB).

The promise of peace is not limited to the human heart—this promise also extends to the nations of the world. Psalm 147:14 states: "He makes peace in your borders."

When the peace of God is released to the borders of nations, wars cease—and new wars are prevented. Internally His peace brings an end to infighting and releases healing through forgiveness. Tranquility and contentment within; security and safety without. Wholeness and completeness for people and nations—nothing missing or lacking, nothing added that does not belong.

That is the sum of *shalom*.

Thank You, Lord, that Your peace is lasting and eternal. I praise You that You bring peace to hearts and peace to nations. Yahweh Shalom, let Your peace break out over all the earth!

May the release of Your peace begin within the walls of Jerusalem and extend outward to the nations of the Middle East. In the center of unrest and conflict, may hearts find their rest and peace in You. Bring reconciliation that lasts—reconciliation made possible by the cross—as hearts are drawn back to You.

Raise up peacemakers in the Middle East who pursue Your peace so they can release it to others. Give them wisdom, understanding and Your supernatural ability to love their enemies. Let nothing interrupt the healing flow of Your love and forgiveness as Your peace makes all complete.

In the powerful name of Jesus, "The LORD Is Peace," I pray this in agreement with Your will in faith. Amen!

Peace That Surpasses All Understanding

She did not start out with perfect peace. Her mind was troubled and her heart was in deep distress.

Ban was a young mother with two children living in Mosul when she learned about ISIS the hard way. Her husband was a taxi driver. One morning he received a call from a Christian family requesting three taxis. He called a few other taxi drivers to help, and they went off to take the assignment. Ban never saw her husband again.

On a side street in Mosul, a group of armed men cornered her husband's taxi. They pulled him from the front seat, placing him in the back of the car with guns pointed at his head. Her husband was kidnapped; the other drivers escaped.

When she learned the news, Ban went to the police station to report the kidnapping. She disguised herself in a *hijab* to hide her identity as a Christian.

The police officer was not surprised at her news. He told her that *Da'esh* (ISIS) was present in that area.

"I don't know this *Da'esh* that you're talking about," Ban told the officer.

The officer explained ISIS was a group, not a person. But Ban was confused. What did they want from her family?

"You will find out soon," he said.

Seven months later, ISIS captured Mosul and made headlines around the world. The international community learned the hard way, too.

A ransom call from the kidnappers came the next day. ISIS wanted $50,000 for the return of her husband—a price she could not pay. When the kidnappers threatened to come after her, too, she grabbed a few clothes and fled to Jordan with her children.

Her life began to spiral out of control.

Ban and her children lived in one room. It was the middle of winter and they were hungry and thirsty and cold. In her misery she reached her breaking point.

"As I grew weak, my faith weakened with me," she said.

Ban slit her wrist and waited to die.

She woke up in the hospital. Her landlord promised to help.

"I had reached a point of hopelessness," Ban said. "I was angry at Jesus. Why did He leave me and my children?"

One cold day in April, Ban accepted the repeated invitation of her landlord to go to church. Though her hopelessness persisted, the Prince of Peace was near.

"I felt the touch of Jesus," Ban explained as she described the moment that changed her life.

Sitting in the church, she heard the pastor say, "Raise your hands. The Lord is near, so raise your hands!" In that moment, Jesus made His presence known.

"I felt such power that I've never felt before. I felt the presence of the Lord," Ban said. "I asked Him to keep me faithful and strong."

And the peace that surpasses all understanding rushed in like a flood, healing her wounded heart.

"The LORD will give strength to His people; the LORD will bless His people with peace" (Psalm 29:11).

On the cold floor of a ward, Betsie lay still on a stretcher. Corrie ten Boom bent down to hear her sister's last words, quietly spoken.

Betsie had survived for nearly nine months through the Holocaust as a prisoner of war, but now the end of her life was near. She was 59 years old, and her body, which had been weakened in the camps, could not withstand much more.

". . . must tell people what we have learned here," she whispered to Corrie. "We must tell them that there is no pit so deep that He is not deeper still."

In death as in life, the power of His peace transcended the pit, turning this loss into glory.

Thank You, Lord, that Your peace is perfect. There is nothing missing or lacking for the one whose mind is focused completely on You. Yahweh Shalom, I declare that You hold an abundance of peace to meet each need for every heart that trusts in You.

Thank You for releasing Your peace over Your people in the Middle East. May Your peace remind them of Your presence. Strengthen them with Your purposes, comfort them with Your protection, encourage them to persevere, inspire their faith as You provide and renew their spirits as You heal.

In the powerful name of Jesus, "The LORD Is Peace," I pray this in agreement with Your will in faith. Amen!

ISIS uses its strategy of savagery to steal the joy, kill the hope and destroy the peace of all within its reach. Jesus warned of a thief like this. He said, "The thief comes only to steal and kill and destroy. I came that they may have life and have it abundantly" (John 10:10 ESV).

Through the power of His name, His love stands in the face of ISIS to redeem what was stolen, revive what was killed and restore what was destroyed.

Proactively, He releases His presence to bring light to the darkness, His armies to fight the battle against evil, His protection to guide and rescue. His banner is raised as it points to the victory of the cross, releasing perseverance to those He loves. He sees ahead to release provision for every need and releases His healing to the brokenhearted, binding up their wounds. Through it all He releases His peace as His blessing of life to all who will call on His name.

This is life that is given abundantly.

This is *Love* that overcomes evil with good.

Out of Your War Room and into the World

Prayer is *powerful*.

When you enter your "war room" to pray—whether that is a literal space or a figurative place in your heart—you attract the attention of God. "When you pray, go into your room, close the door and pray to your Father, who is unseen. Then your Father, who sees what is done in secret, will reward you" (Matthew 6:6 NIV). As you draw near to God, He draws near to you.

Prayer is an intentional act of faith that delights His soul.

God desires to hear *your* voice as you speak to Him in prayer. David knew this best. Nearly a dozen instances are recorded in the Psalms where David affirms the benefit of praying aloud with his voice, that God may hear. "Evening and morning and at noon I will pray, and cry aloud, and He shall hear my voice" (Psalm 55:17).

There is nothing wrong with quiet prayers or the meditations of your heart that are focused on the Lord. Hannah prayed fervently in this way when she was desperate to bear a son. Eli, the priest, misunderstood her grief and thought she was drunk. God received her prayer and granted her request (see 1 Samuel 1). Before a single word is spoken, God knows the thoughts and intentions of your heart.

Yet there is something powerful that happens when you use your voice to pray aloud and cry out to the Lord. These are the prayers of intense desire that signal defeat to the enemy as they move the heart of God.

He felt the ground beneath him shaking like an earthquake. He heard an incredible roar. For a brief moment, he wondered if a bomb were exploding. Neither scenario was correct.

Sujo John was standing just a few feet away from the South Tower of the World Trade Center on September 11, 2001, when the building began to collapse. Having miraculously escaped down a stairwell from his burning office on the 81st floor of the North Tower, the first tower struck, and now standing between the two, he watched helplessly as the South Tower began to fall.

He was not watching the terrible scene alone. Sujo and about twenty other people were huddled together against a wall. He heard the voice of the Lord speak clearly to his heart: *Where are these people you see going without Me?*

A boldness came over Sujo. No longer afraid of what people might think, he began to cry out the name of Jesus. To his surprise, Sujo began to hear their cries to Jesus mingled with his own.

They prayed for what seemed like a few minutes, until the deafening noise of the building imploding silenced their cries. As the building came down, Sujo fell, with his face flat on the ground. He thought he was going to die.

Buried under soot, ash and debris, Sujo was able to crawl out, but he soon realized that of those in the group he alone had survived the disaster. He did not understand why the others had died. They had called on the name of the Lord, just as he had. In that moment, the Lord answered him.

"I felt this peace from heaven," Sujo said. "The Bible gives us the assurance that to be absent in the body is to be present with Jesus."[1]

The power of one person's voice spoken aloud in prayer influenced the eternal destinies of those who heard him that fateful day.

Scripture gives many examples of the strength of one person's prayer. Daniel knelt down in prayer to God three times a day—and through this, God found him blameless. When Daniel would not alter his prayer life to satisfy the order of the king, he was thrown into a den of ravenous lions. God sent angels to shut the mouths of the lions, and Daniel survived unharmed.

Daniel's lifestyle of continual prayer released God's help in his time of need.

Jesus often prayed alone. Before He chose the inner circle of men who would become His apostles, He went up to the mountain and prayed throughout the night. When day came, He called out to the Twelve to join Him—then He went down to the crowd to heal all who sought a touch from Him (see Luke 6:12–19).

"The prayer of a righteous person is powerful and effective" (James 5:16 NIV).

Where Two or Three Are Gathered

They were thrown into a "war room" of a different kind—the inner cell of a prison, where their feet were fastened in stocks.

Paul and Silas had come to the city of Philippi. A slave girl controlled by a demon of divination followed them for many days. She brought her owners much financial gain by her fortune telling. Though her words were accurate, Paul became greatly annoyed and cast out the evil spirit in the name of Jesus Christ. For this action, both he and Silas were brought before the rulers and flogged—severely beaten with many blows—then thrown into prison.

What does not kill you can make your spirit stronger, when the Lord is at your side.

At midnight, Paul and Silas were heard praying aloud and singing hymns by the prisoners who were listening to them. Though bloodied and beaten, their spirits were not broken. They understood the power of praise, worship and spoken prayer.

Their worship and prayers released the response of heaven. "Suddenly, there was a massive earthquake, and the prison was shaken to its foundations. All the doors immediately flew open, and the chains of every prisoner fell off!" (Acts 16:26 NLT).

What an amazing demonstration of the power of prayer!

Jesus taught about the power of prayer through the agreement of two or three people. "Again I say to you that if two of you agree on earth concerning anything that they ask, it will be done for them by My Father in heaven. For where two or three are gathered together in My name, I am there in the midst of them" (Matthew 18:19–20).

There is strength released through unity when two or more come together to pray. Praying with others may be a new experience for you or an activity that comes quite easily. I encourage you to find someone you trust who shares this desire to pray over the situation in the Middle East. Pray together regularly.

There are many ways to put this into action. You might want to invite a friend to join you in your home, using the prayers in this book as a place to start. Or you might prefer to go out and walk in your neighborhood, taking turns to pray for the needs as you focus on the promises of God. Who knows—your prayer walks might just catch on and inspire others to join you!

Unity in Prayer

The early Church was devoted to prayer, united in one purpose. The book of Acts describes how they took this privilege seriously and made it their priority. As a result the presence of God descended and the power of God was released— power given to them to be His bold witnesses to the ends of the earth.

The Church has been given a mandate to pray. In her book *The Power of Praying Together* (Harvest House, 2003), Stormie Omartian shares an insight from her pastor, Jack Hayford, on corporate prayer: "One of the hindrances to intercessory prayer is ignorance of the church's collective mission, which is the call to prayer." These words were spoken more than a decade ago.

The time of ignorance is over.

It is time to reignite the passion within the Church to carry Jesus' compassion through prayer. Your church can adopt a city in the Middle East and pray for the challenges it faces. Learn about its history so that you can learn about its destiny. Pay attention to the news to understand its specific needs. As you pray together for these concerns, ask God to reveal the ways in which He has answered your prayers—then watch your faith grow and get bolder still.

What are the intangibles that make for a successful time of corporate prayer?

First, it is essential that good leadership is in place. This means that the leader has clear vision for the purpose of the time spent together, and those participating recognize and respect his or her leadership. This vision for the group needs to be articulated clearly, so that all members understand their individual purposes in prayer and place high value on their time spent together.

Next, there must be unity within the group—one focus, one desire, one passion. In any gathering, there will be a variety of topics to pray about, and it is easy to get sidetracked. With so many areas to pray over this situation in the Middle East, the leader might want to choose one specific topic per meeting to focus on and communicate that goal to the group ahead of time. This allows group members the opportunity to ask the Lord for specific insight, before coming together to pray. Creating a Facebook group for your members is a great way to keep the prayer focus strong from week to week, as well as provide an avenue to support prayer requests and share relevant information on current events as they unfold.

As your group prays, remember that your words spoken in agreement with God's heart are powerful. You are not speaking empty words, but are communicating with the living God—so be intentional with what you present to Him. Come before Him with great expectation!

A successful time of corporate prayer will include times of praise and worship, because worship and intercession are intertwined. They are hard to separate one from the other when the Spirit is moving. Praise is your declaration, which becomes your prayer that leads you into worship—and let the cycle begin again.

Finally, ask the Lord if He would choose *you* to be the one to lead your church or community group to pray for the crisis in the Middle East. Don't be afraid! To those He calls, He enables. You will not be going forward alone.

Now is a good time to start!

MY PRAYER FOR YOU

Thank You, Lord, for imparting Your heart of compassion to those who are reading these words right now. Thank You for stirring in them the desire to pray for the people and the nations of the Middle East that have been torn apart by the atrocities of ISIS. Keep their hearts sensitive to the needs of others as they keep their eyes focused on You.

Ignite a flame in their hearts that will draw others to join them in prayer. May they come before You boldly in faith, as they pray in agreement with Your will. Create opportunities for them to inspire groups and churches to do the same.

Release Your presence over them as they pray. Quicken their hearts as they pray over the nations of the Middle East, guiding them with new strategies in prayer. Give them endurance to "pray without ceasing" each time that You call them to pray. Provide them with new insight into Your purposes, filling them with all they need. Release Your healing through the words they speak as You wrap them in Your peace.

In the powerful name of Jesus, "The Prince of Peace," I pray this in agreement with Your will in faith. Amen!

Afterword

Recommended Organizations

Christians often express frustration when faced with a crisis of the magnitude of ISIS in the Middle East. Horrified by news reports, many want to help but feel powerless to effect any real change in countries so distant from their own.

You are different. You have been empowered with prayer strategies to release the authority and power of heaven into the crisis—strategies that can and will make a difference.

As part of your spiritual warfare, you might want to pray for specific organizations that are fighting in the trenches in the Middle East. I mention here three that are doing tremendous humanitarian work. They provide food, housing, education, medical services and more to meet the growing needs of displaced and refugee families. Information given through their websites, blogs and newsletters can help direct you in your prayers. You can also follow each of these organizations on Facebook and share status updates with your friends. This can be a wonderful way to increase awareness of the crisis and help build prayer support.

The Foundation for Relief and Reconciliation in the Middle East (FRRME) helps Christian Iraqi refugees in Jordan and Internally Displaced Persons in Iraq and Kurdistan by providing shelter and medical care, along with education for the children.

> Website: www.frrme.org
> Website: www.frrmeamerica.org
> Facebook: www.facebook.com/FRRME
> Facebook: www.facebook.com/americanfrrme

Preemptive Love Coalition (PLC) provides food and shelter to families persecuted by extremists and education for the children. PLC also provides heart surgeries for children in the Middle East and small business empowerment grants.

> Website: www.preemptivelove.org
> Facebook: www.facebook.com/preemptivelove

Iraqi Children Foundation (ICF) assists orphans and other vulnerable children in Iraq. ICF also provides funding for a children's center in Baghdad that gives nutritious meals, tutoring, health care and more.

> Website: sicfiraq.org
> Facebook: www.facebook.com/IraqiChildrenFoundation

Notes

Introduction

1. "Militants Seize Iraq's Second City of Mosul," *BBC News*, June 10, 2014, http://www.bbc.com/news/world-middle-east-27778112.
2. Alissa J. Rubin, "ISIS Forces Last Iraqi Christians to Flee Mosul," *New York Times*, July 18, 2014, http://www.nytimes.com/2014/07/19/world/middle east/isis-forces-last-iraqi-christians-to-flee-mosul.html.
3. Kelly Phillips Erb, "Islamic State Warns Christians: Convert, Pay Tax, Leave or Die," *Forbes*, July 19, 2014, http://www.forbes.com/sites/kellyphillipserb/201 4/07/19/islamic-state-warns-christians-convert-pay-tax-leave-or-die/.
4. Christine Sisto, "A Christian Genocide Symbolized by One Letter," *National Review*, July 23, 2014, http://www.nationalreview.com/article/383493/christian -genocide-symbolized-one-letter-christine-sisto.
5. Rebecca Perring, "Why Are Facebook and Twitter Users Changing Their Profile Pictures to an Arabic Symbol?" *Express*, July 24, 2014, http://www.express .co.uk/news/world/491391/Online-symbol-of-solidarity-after-ISIS-tell-Iraqi-Ch ristians-to-convert-pay-or-face-death.
6. Dr. Bryant G. Wood, "What Is the Significance of Iraq in the Bible?" *Christian Answers Network*, http://christiananswers.net/q-abr/abr-iraq.html.
7. "Jews in Islamic Countries: Iraq," *Jewish Virtual Library*, https://www.jewish virtuallibrary.org/jsource/anti-semitism/iraqijews.html.
8. Raya Jalabi, "Who Are the Yazidis and Why Are ISIS Hunting Them?" *Guardian*, August 11, 2014, http://www.theguardian.com/world/2014/aug/07/who -yazidi-isis-iraq-religion-ethnicity-mountains.
9. Jessica Stern and J.M. Berger, "Thugs Wanted—Bring Your Own Boots: How ISIS Attracts Foreign Fighters to Its Twisted Utopia," *Guardian*, March 9, 2015, http://www.theguardian.com/world/2015/mar/09/how-isis-attracts-foreign -fighters-the-state-of-terror-book.

10. Graeme Wood, "What ISIS's Leader Really Wants," *New Republic*, September 1, 2014, http://www.newrepublic.com/article/119259/isis-history-islamic-states-new-caliphate-syria-and-iraq.

11. Itai Zehorai, "The Word's 10 Richest Terrorist Organizations," *Forbes*, December 12, 2014, http://www.forbes.com/sites/forbesinternational/2014/12/12/the-worlds-10-richest-terrorist-organizations/.

12. Mark Durie, "A Message Signed with Blood to the Nation of the Cross," February 21, 2015, http://blog.markdurie.com/2015/02/a-message-signed-with-blood-to-nation.html.

Chapter 1: Your First Line of Defense

1. Grant R. Osborne, "Luke 17," in *Intervarsity Press New Testament Commentaries*, https://www.biblegateway.com/resources/commentaries/IVP-NT/Luke/Faithful-Looking-King-Kingdom.

2. Translations of biblical Greek and Hebrew words are taken from *BlueLetter Bible.org*, http://www.blueletterbible.org/lang/lexicon/lexicon.cfm?Strongs.

Chapter 3: Pray to Release the Presence of God

1. Bill Hutchinson, "ISIS Fighters Coming to Christ and Nepal Earthquake Relief Work," *Youth With A Mission Podcast*, June 10, 2015, http://ywampodcast.com/isis-fighters-coming-to-christ-and-nepal-earthquake-relief-work/.

2. Andrew White, *Faith Under Fire* (Oxford: Monarch Books, 2011), 119.

Chapter 4: Pray to Release the Armies of God

1. Jessica Stern and J.M. Berger, *ISIS: The State of Terror* (New York: HarperCollins, 2015), 23.

2. Todd Nettleton, "Muslim Finds Christ: I'm Sick of Killing," *Voice of the Martyrs Radio*, July 2, 2015, https://secure.persecution.com/radio/default.aspx?pdid=6230.

3. Ibid.

Chapter 5: Pray to Release the Protection of God

1. Ed Payne, "ISIS Takes Strategically Important Town in Western Syria, Rights Group Says," *CNN*, August 7, 2015, http://www.cnn.com/2015/08/07/world/syria-isis-al-qaryatayn-christians/.

2. French Agency Press, "ISIS Kidnaps 230 Civilians in Central Syria," *Daily Star Lebanon*, August 7, 2015, http://www.dailystar.com.lb/News/Middle-East/2015/Aug-07/310098-isis-militants-abduct-dozens-of-christians-including-woman-and-children-after-taking-town-in.ashx.

3. Sam Webb, "ISIS Takes 'Prettiest Virgins' as Sex Slaves and Burned One Alive for Refusing Extreme Perverted Acts," *Mirror UK*, May 20, 2015, http://www.mirror.co.uk/news/world-news/isis-take-prettiest-virgins-sex-5728456.

4. Sue Lloyd-Roberts, "Raped, Beaten and Sold: Yazidi Women Tell of IS Abuse," *BBC Newsnight*, July 14, 2015, http://www.bbc.com/news/world-mid dle-east-33522204.

Chapter 6: Pray to Release Perseverance for the People of God

1. Rosalie Hughes, "A Crisis of Anxiety Among Aid Workers," *New York Times*, March 8, 2015, http://www.nytimes.com/2015/03/09/opinion/a-crisis-of -anxiety-among-aid-workers.html.

2. Stefan Lovgren, "Aid Workers, Too, Suffering Post-Traumatic Stress," *National Geographic News*, December 3, 2003, http://news.nationalgeographic.com /news/2003/12/1203_031203_aidworkers_2.html.

3. Lela Gilbert, *Saturday People, Sunday People* (New York: Encounter Books, 2012), 154.

Chapter 7: Pray to Release the Provision of God

1. David A. Graham, "Violence Has Forced 60 Million People from Their Homes," *The Atlantic*, June 17, 2015, http://www.theatlantic.com/international /archive/2015/06/refugees-global-peace-index/396122/; Orlando Crowcroft, "ISIS: Worst Refugee Crisis in a Generation as Millions Flee Islamic State in Iraq and Syria," *International Business Times*, June 17, 2015, http://www.ibtimes.co.uk/isis -worst-refugee-crisis-generation-millions-flee-islamic-state-iraq-syria-1506613.

2. Ann Voskamp, "Into Iraq #1: Love in the Time of ISIS," *A Holy Experience*, April 16, 2015, http://www.aholyexperience.com/2015/04/into-iraq-1-love -in-the-time-of-isis/.

3. For a description of the fast the Lord desires, see Isaiah 58.

Chapter 8: Pray to Release the Healing of God

1. Susanne Babbel Ph.D., M.F.T., "The Connections Between Emotional Stress, Trauma and Physical Pain," *Psychology Today*, April 8, 2010, https://www.psych ologytoday.com/blog/somatic-psychology/201004/the-connections-between -emotional-stress-trauma-and-physical-pain.

2. Liz Ford, "Yazidi's Yearn for Their Sinjar Home One Year After ISIS Forced Them to Flee," *Guardian*, August 3, 2015, http://www.theguardian.com/global -development/2015/aug/03/yazidis-sinjar-iraq-one-year-anniversary-isis.

3. Loveday Morris, "Iraqi Yazidis Stranded on Isolated Mountaintop Begin to Die of Thirst," *Washington Post*, August 5, 2014, https://www.washingtonpost .com/world/iraqi-yazidis-stranded-on-isolated-mountaintop-begin-to-die-of -thirst/2014/08/05/57cca985–3396–41bd-8163–7a52e5e72064_story.html.

4. Rukmini Callimachi, "ISIS Enshrines a Theology of Rape," *New York Times*, August 13, 2015, http://www.nytimes.com/2015/08/14/world/middleeast /isis-enshrines-a-theology-of-rape.html.

5. Ibid.

6. Ibid.

7. Judith Herman, M.D., *Trauma and Recovery* (New York: Basic Books, 1992), 52–55.

8. See 1 Samuel 17:34–37; 1 Samuel 21:10–15; 1 Samuel 22; 2 Samuel 16:11; 2 Samuel 18:32–33; 2 Samuel 21:15–17.

Chapter 9: Pray to Release the Peace of God

1. Jimmy Draper, "Call to Prayer: Persecution from a Chinese Christian's Perspective," *Baptist Press*, May 30, 2014, http://www.bpnews.net/42677/call-to-prayer-persecution-from-a-chinese-christians-perspective.

Chapter 10: Out of Your War Room and into the World

1. Charlene Aaron, "Sept. 11 Survivor: 'My Life Has Totally Changed,'" *CBN News*, September 11, 2012, http://www.cbn.com/cbnnews/us/2009/September/911-Survivor-Shares-Survival-Story/.

Lorraine Marie Varela is a professional portrait photographer, author and lifelong follower of Jesus. Her first book, *Powerful Moments in the Presence of God* (Chosen, 2015), combines her photography with words of hope, inspiring readers to draw near to the heart of God and personally experience the awe of being in His presence.

In the summer of 2015, Lorraine and her husband, Gabriel, traveled to the Middle East to meet Iraqi Christian refugees who fled their country when ISIS commanded the world stage—a time to listen, to learn, to pray. In this life-changing encounter, Lorraine heard the stories of her Iraqi brothers and sisters and was startled to realize their lives mirrored her own. Their stories could be her story one day. Lorraine returned home with fresh revelation of God's heart of love for the people and the region of the Middle East. She carries a strong desire to share God's passion for people and to encourage believers everywhere to pray.

Lorraine lives in the Seattle area, where she has operated a boutique portrait photography studio for the past ten years. She is involved in leadership at Beit Tikvah House of Hope, a Foursquare Messianic congregation in Newcastle, Washington. Lorraine and Gabriel have two grown daughters.

To connect with Lorraine, you can find her online:

www.LorraineMarie.com
www.Facebook.com/InspiringFaithwithLorraineVarela
www.Twitter.com/LMVarela

Refresh Your Soul Today

You can experience the incredible joy of hearing God's voice and experiencing His love in a personal, life-transforming way—every day. These inspiring thoughts and corresponding Scriptures, accompanied by the author's spectacular photography, take only moments to read, but they will renew your mind, refocus your heart and usher you into the presence of the Almighty.

Come expectantly!

"A work of art."
—**Randy Clark**

"What a pleasure. You will be richer for it."
—**Luci Swindoll**

Powerful Moments in the Presence of God
by Lorraine Marie Varela